Career Development

Designing Self

John H. Peatling
    Director of Basic Research
    Union College
    Character Research Project
    Schenectady, New York

David V. Tiedeman
    Professor of Education
    Northern Illinois University
    DeKalb, Illinois

Accelerated Development Inc.
P. O. Box 667
Muncie, Indiana 47305

Library of Congress Catalog Card Number: 77-72213

International Standard Book Number: 0-915202-09-3

Corporate Editor: Linda K. Davis

Cover Design: Mary Blizzard

Printed in the United States of America
June 1977

For additional copies order from

Accelerated Development Inc.
Publication Division
P. O. Box 667
Muncie, Indiana 47305

Cost $9.95 plus postage and handling
                in U. S. and Canada add 50 cents
                in other countries, postage depends upon
                    prevailing rates

Price is subject to change without notice.

This work is about knowing. In one way or another we have encountered the epistemological question. We tend to agree with Jean Piaget that, "The basic epistemological alternatives are predestination or some sort of constructivism" (Piaget, 1968/1971, p. 141). Given that alternative, we opt for constructivism or, as we call it, a constructionist position.

We are persuaded that each man and woman is a researcher. Therefore, we understand education as a relationship between a person and the environment which allows a person to master what he or she investigates. In the course of such an investigation a person engages in the process of self-construction or, as some would say, becoming (Combs, 1962, p. 234ff.).

We also are persuaded that currently available analogs can enable men and women to comprehend even such complexities as the Self. We invoke the complex analog of the electronic computer and the unfamiliar but very useful theory of mathematical groups. We also offer a design for three successively more complex interactive Information Systems for Vocational Decisions, Education Decisions, and Self Decisions. The first of these Information Systems has worked; the second we illustrate with our own processes of discovery; the third we propose as a next step in the construction of human beings.

We have tried to treat a complex subject with some precision. We have tried to make what we are doing abundantly evident, for we are interested in a process of knowing that culminates in comprehension. However, we suspect that our readers may represent a complex of interests, needs, and desires. Therefore, we urge them to consider how to approach this work.

Our text is divided into three sections, each of which begins with an overview, which contains a rationale for what we have to say in that section. One way to survey our work is to read the overviews of the three sections sequentially.

In Section I is proposed the design of an Education Machine, using the electronic computer as an analog. In Section II is offered an extended example of an interchange with such an Education Machine on the subject of human personality. Section II contains an example of what was designed in Section I as a process to achieve personal knowing through research, a process regarded as quintessentially educational. In Section III is proposed the development of a Self Machine, which would use discoveries from Section II as a person-serving prosthetic device for self-controlled construction of personality. Section III concludes with a proposal for development of what we choose to call a Self Research Machine Game.

Although backgrounds of the authors are rather different, we agree upon some basic conclusions. We value Mankind, and we believe in both human freedom and human dignity. We also are concerned that Mankind be responsible. We think that to see Mankind as a construction can lead to freedom, dignity, and responsibility. We are optimistic about what Mankind may be. We hope that our readers will share our optimism, as they comprehend the complexity of the processes which result in construction of human personality.

Finally, we think that we have been fundamentally scientific in our approach to Mankind as Knower and as a Self under construction (Tiedeman, 1960, p. 486). However, we also are aware that Thompson's phrase--"What one fool can do, another can"--is true of what we have accomplished. Therefore, through whatever approach readers encounter our work, we strongly suspect that most will discover that they can do what we have done. If they reach this conclusion, we will be pleased, for we would regard such a result as a great reward for our efforts.

John H. Peatling
David V. Tiedeman

April 1977

CONTENTS

LIST OF FIGURES

LIST OF TABLES

ACKNOWLEDGMENTS

The authors gratefully acknowledge permission to use materials previously published. We particularly wish to thank the following for allowing us to use material already copyrighted: the College Entrance Examination Board for permission to use material from D. V. Tiedeman and R. P. O'Hara, Career Development: Choice and Adjustment (1963); the Union College Character Research Project for permission to reproduce the two tables found in Figure 3.1 and 3.2, and to quote from Character Potential: A Record of Research (Vol. 5, Nos 1 & 2, July, 1970); John R. Platt for permission to quote from his work, Hierarchical Restructuring (1970); the publishers of MIND, Basil Blackwell and Mott Ltd., for permission to use Turing's quotation; the Center for Research on Learning and Teaching for permission to use the quotation from Karl L. Zinn and Susan McClintock, which comes from a preliminary form of their paper, "Instructional Use of Computers: A Critical Examination With Recommendations for Action," which was published in World Conference on Computer Education, 1970, (Amsterdam: International Federation for Information Processing, 1971); and Robert J. Seidel, Program Director Instructional Technology, Human Resources Research Organization, for permission to quote his description of Project IMPACT use of "instructional decision models."

As the reader will readily detect, we also owe intellectual debts to a number of persons whose thinking and writing helped us reach the place we now are. We think particularly of Alan M. Turing, Ivor A. Richards, Michael Polanyi, Robert P. O'Hara, R. Buckminister Fuller, Jean Piaget, Herbert Simon, Clare W. Graves, Ann Roe, Ernest M. Ligon, Jerome Bruner and B. F. Skinner. Undoubtedly there also are many others. However, while our debt is real enough, the results are ours and no one need feel responsible for how their work has been used, interpreted, or transformed by us. That is solely our responsibility. In addition, we acknowledge encouragement and help of our friends and families, whose patience and insight have been so readily available to us as we have taken this intellectual journey.

* * * * * * * * * * * * * * * *

SECTION I

AN OVERVIEW

* * * * * * * * * * * * * * * *

.

SECTION I

AN OVERVIEW

Silvanus Thompson (1946) introduced his little book, Calculus Made Easy, with the inscription, "What one fool can do, another can." These words proved startling enough to one of us, who had struggled through The Calculus several years before, to cause him to reconfront The Calculus through Thompson. The years, circumstances, or Thompson made The Calculus easier on the second exposure.

Therefore, we dedicate this work to what we would term "Thompson's Principle." We thoroughly believe that a reader can do what we can do. Since we consider ourselves "fools," as Thompson did, we tar our readers with the brush as well. But do not let us, thereby, put anyone off. As you read this, we feel certain it will project our strong and sincere belief that not only you can do what we can do but also you may do it even better! This hope seems to us to be the essence of true scholarship, to which we unashamedly aspire.

Contrary to popular opinion, Knowledge is _not_ something inscribed on tablets or, even, written in books and available only to an annointed few who can understand the fruits of another's scholarship. Rather, we believe that Knowledge is the personal result of the engagement of one's mind with one's environment in an attitude of wanting to know. Thus, Knowledge is the personal product of the act of knowing.

This work is about knowing--the attitude and habit of knowing--and about the relationship one should build between oneself and one's environment, to help one master what is investigated. In Section I is presented a design for knowing which may be unfamiliar, but we hope that it will be understood. Essentially, we wish to dispel public "worship" of the products of another's research and, then, to seek credibility for the proposition that each of us bears in his or her personhood the essential capacity for research. Actualization, rather than crippling, of that capacity should characterize life.

In seeking credibility for the proposition that each of us can be, or _is_, essentially, a researcher, we question a well-established educational "shibboleth." That shibboleth regards Knowledge as something outside learners that is to be put into

them, rather than something that is inside the learners that is
to be brought forth from them. The design we propose for the
bringing forth of Knowledge is that of an Education Machine.
In proposing this design, which at the moment we can sketch
only incompletely, we choose to use the computing machine analog. We have chosen this particular device because in designing a machine one formalizes a set of procedures which a machine
repeats to fulfill the functions one wants it to perform.

In Section I we try to design a machine that will dis-
charge the functions we expect, rather than do just what men
and women usually do. We want to avoid the error of making our
educational design into the image of existing Mankind, but
devoid of our intentions for an educational design.

After we propose a design for an Education Machine that we
believe will facilitate achievement of a belief in Self as
Knower, we illustrate how we have acted as Knowers in the realm
of Personality. We do that in Section II. In Section III we
conclude with what we take to be our essential purpose, to present a design of Self. What we want to propose is that a person
can apply our first proposition (i.e. Self is a Knower) to
knowing personality as the group construct that we propose it
to be. We think persons who gain that comprehension will be
empowered to know their own personhood by letting "personalities" develop through the group structure we outline in Section II. Thus, Section I is a first step, a beginning, down a
pathway we believe is an important one to travel.

CHAPTER 1

RESEARCH AND AN EDUCATION MACHINE

THE GAP BETWEEN RESEARCH AND EDUCATION

Research and education logically are different. However, we argue that modern computers create the possibility for individual citizens to bridge this logical gap and to do so in a way that eliminates the now potential threat to individual freedom inherent in this gap's existence. The value of our argument rests not only in offering a resolution to a perplexing and logical problem. It has further value because, in a period of increasing polarization of students, government, and parents, the argument offers an alternative that should be considered very carefully.

The distance between research and education is manifested presently as a crisis in support of educational research, to say nothing of a crisis in support of the educational venture itself. People in Congress now expect educational research to modify education itself. Yet, these same congresspeople frequently forget that requiring such results from educational research demands that the congresspeople themselves must assume responsibility for a shift in goals, policies, and organization of financial and personnel resources. Such shifts must occur when either new ends or new means are introduced.

The Congress of the United States of America is the only analog that exists of a Federal School Committee, or a Federal Board of Regents. Unfortunately, the present political crisis vis-a-vis education is aggravated further by the fact that the U. S. Commissioner of Education and the counterparts in both state and local school systems fail to attempt a continually revised but comprehensive organization of research. As a result, the needed policy implications and changes are <u>not</u> obvious to those who must bring the changes into reality. This situation has little chance of changing as long as the direct attention of the Congress and other policy-making bodies is lacking such as it now seems to be.

Both student unrest and student quietism bring the logical gap between research and education closer to center stage. The eternal separation of generations is even greater than is the political separation of policy and administration. The old will never be young again. Yet, if an understanding is to be achieved between the generations, the new thinking of the young must perpetually find accommodation in the previous thinking of the old, with the reverse also being true. Restless or quiet, students presently demand that their education be relevant. Inherent in that demand is their assumption that individual and comprehensive understanding of a subject, of themselves, of their learning, and of their thought-grounded processes of acting is not only possible but necessary.

The gap between research and education seems to be perpetuated almost deliberately by educational researchers. However, we argue that it is the gap itself that aggravates students. The aggravated students seem to want their education guided by the most immediate and best understandings of how the marvelously plastic human spirit can be guided toward more mature comprehension of individual responsibility for action based on understanding. Yet, neither educator nor educational researcher provides these students with either the belief or the expectation that comprehensively understood maturation is possible. Nor do we provide students with the feasible and dynamic systems which can synergize interactions with devices designed to produce thought-grounded action.

But, must a gap between research and education exist? The answer reverberating throughout our present systems of thought seems to be an unequivocal, YES! This answer presumes that that in which something is grounded always has precedence over that which it directs. Given our present systems of thought, that conviction dictates an inevitable gap between research and education. However, a dynamic interaction with the states and properties relevant for knowing is now within reach of Every Person.

Unfortunately, the United States of America seems to consider attainment of that reach not economically feasible. Perhaps the conclusion results from an apprehensive concern about whether people ever can have, or ever should have, a societally confirmable and confirmed belief in a capacity to know and to live comprehensively. Yet, we contend that projection of just such an attitude of doubt is what annoys young people, since our doubts are not confirmed by their experiences. Young people continually are close to multi-purposed, interactive forms of thinking and living, forms in which they encounter new

8

problems, new possibilities, and new means that, to their certain knowledge, exist. For the young, they exist; for those of us who are older, however, they do not.

That is why we propose publicly to re-examine our "old" thinking; we want to determine whether the new thinking has a place in our systems of thinking and believing. We trust that _our_ re-examination gives youth some measure of hope, no matter how small, that _their_ new desires and new possibilities may be reflected in _our_ old learning. We suspect that we will not please youth fully. After all, new thinking which emerges from old thinking rarely is fully consonant with new thinking itself. However, we hope that our effort may have an effect upon even our outraged critics. The effect we hope for is synergistic; that is, the result may give us both, old and young, a base from which we can work together toward the further modification of old thinking into more appropriately based forms of new thinking.

PIERS OF A POTENTIAL BRIDGE BETWEEN RESEARCH AND EDUCATION: THE POSSIBILITY OF AN EDUCATING RESEARCH MACHINE

We seek an _individual_ bridging of the gap between research and education. Therefore, we ask, "What resources do we now have that might serve as piers in a potential individual bridging of the gap between research and education?"

Several consolidated sets, or "packages," of computer programs were developed during the 1960's (e.g., Colley and Lohnes, 1962) and exist today (e.g., Dixon, _BMD Biomedical Computer Programs,_ 1968, 1969). These packages of computer programs tie together a number of statistical procedures and permit three important things to happen. First, the designation (on a fairly general basis) of a particular sub-set of the total set of programs that an investigator wants to use can be made. Second, in the sub-set of programs the investigator can then introduce his or her own designation of the variables and data that are to be used. Third, within a generally preconceived pattern, reports are constructed that are specific to the particular variables and data the investigator has supplied. Such a rudimentary, albeit dynamic, use of statistical programs in numerical analysis is now fairly routine in computers used in a batch processing or manually job-qued mode. Obviously these programs need some way to inform their users when variable designations or data fail to conform to their preprogrammed assumptions. As a commonplace example of such a procedure, who has not heard the taped voice of an operator interrupt one's wait for a directly dialed long-distance number with the message, "You have failed to dial enough digits. Please hang up and dial again"? Therefore, most statistical analysis packages now contain error messages, from which the program chooses and prints the appropriate response when one of the program's necessary restraints is not fulfilled in the specific instance.

Investigators now using such packages occasionally expect one kind of analysis, fail to get it, and receive advice (error messages and diagnostics) as to why the investigators' preconceived notions may not have materialized. These occurrences are more than just annoying; they create an interaction of an investigator with his or her own forms of thought and data. As a result of this interaction, an investigator can adapt the process to achieve a more satisfactory compliance with his or her desires and, so, receive reports which add credibility to results.

Steps in Augmenting One's Power to Relate Machine Design and Data

Given the experiential background, one can imagine the first step in an approach to a dynamic relationship between machine design and data in educational research. However, the time interval between the initial request and a revised request needs to be reduced sufficiently to give an investigator the impression that he or she is interacting creatively with the data. Although using a program package's capacity to achieve such dynamic interrelationships is expensive, since the computer is being used in what is called a time-sharing mode, the capacity for that dynamic relationship presently does exist and, in some places, can even be purchased on the open market.

A second step in augmenting one's power to relate machine design and data in more dynamic, effective ways has been made possible by programming the computer so that data may be updated between requests for re-analyses. These even more expensive uses of the computer are, currently, largely limited to investigations in the physical sciences in which risk to life is great. Examples are investigations involving linear acceleration of atoms and transport of man to and from the vastness of space. However, in education uses made of these computational forms are limited essentially to updating pupil or other informational records (e.g., college or occupational opportunities). Such updating as presently exists usually occurs on waves of long amplitude and, therefore, usually utilizes a computer programmed for batch processing, not for time-sharing. Nevertheless, we do have the basic technology for developing educational data files. Also the technology for actively maintaining such files is somewhat developed and continues to be developed. As this technology is developed further, one will be even more able to sustain the illusion that one is dealing with data in or of motion. As this process becomes possible, interactions will permit one to impose design upon data in

appropriate ways. An example of such a development is M.I.T.'s
Project Cambridge, which increases even more fully the interactive possibilities of form and data.

A third step in augmenting one's power to relate machine
design and data in ever more dynamic and individually determined fashions was provided by the prototype of Hutchinson
(1968). A general object of what is called discriminant analysis is the ability to ascertain the group from which a particular set of scores is most likely to have been drawn (Rulon,
Tiedeman, Tatsuoka and Langmuir, 1967). Hutchinson combined
this general capability, in a computer environment, with the
capability of defining groups as one sees fit, within certain
previously determined limits. This new union of possibilities
enables the user, in a few programmed instances, first to indicate what he or she values among accomplishments of other researchers and, then, to ascertain whether characteristics they
identified as prerequisite are similar to those needed in his
of her group. In general, this capability contains the rudimentary means to re-allocate sets of data to new categories
and, then, to perform analyses designed along dimensions of the
re-defined data.

Designs for Dynamic Interactions in Instruction

Discriminant analysis is one giant step in the evolving
potential of an individualized, interactive bridging of the gap
between research and education. Now let us move from designs
for dynamic interactions with numeric data to designs for dynamic interactions in instruction.

Development of instructional programming during the decade
of the 1950's led in the 1960's to development of various forms
of computer-aided and computer-assisted aids to instruction.
Zinn and McClintock of the University of Michigan have completed for publication a final report of Project CLUE (Computer
Learning Under Evaluation). We need not dwell on the content
that report covers, but we do want to refer to the preliminary
report (Zinn and McClintock, 1970) by citing five guises in
which the computer presently figures in education: computer-
aided or computer-assisted instruction; computer-based instruction; computer-managed instruction; computer-aided learning;
and, what these authors termed, computer-aided education. More
than a mere play on words exists in these five guises, for, as
Zinn and McClintock noted, the role of the computer in education varies in these five guises according to (a) the amount
and kind of program control available to the person, (b) the
program's use of diagnosis and prescription, (c) the variety of
computer functions made directly available to the user, (d) the
type of interaction, (e) the role of the computer for

individual services, and (f) the "naturalness" of the communication between learner and system.

Zinn and McClintock (1970) further explained these trends, in which the role of the computer is being shifted in education, as follows:

A major trend in design of computer-based exercises is a shift from program to learner control. The designer of the exercises is putting less energy into a careful diagnosis and prescription accomplished by some automated instructional strategy and more effort into providing information from which the student can assemble his specific prescription.

Most systems and lesson designers are providing an increasing variety of functions for the user of the learning system. More attention is being given to interaction, not simply how quickly a reply can be made to some question, but the actual responsiveness of the system to the particular input. This means that machine responses are increasingly dependent upon the commands and questions and answers typed by the student, and the lessons are designed in a way that the student is more likely to respond to information provided by the computer.

A very important trend concerns the role of the machine from the perspective of the individual using it. The teacher is now more likely to see computer-managed instruction as an aid to human management than as a replacement for it. Probably much more important, learners find the machine more suitable as an aid to learning than as a drill master.

Naturalness of communication between learner and system is being improved day by day. Computer-based learning exercises are achieving increased relevance for the subject being studied, and the nomenclature and conventions that have to be learned to use the system tend to be essential to the study of the topics (apart from the requirements of the computer as a medium of presentation). (Zinn & McClintock, 1970, Appendix D, pp. 15-16)

Zinn and McClintock's statements indicated that the computer creates a union of design and instruction within which one can now imagine sets representative of the processes of education. Zinn and McClintock provided a dynamic form of the process in the summary of their work in Project CLUE. In the following excerpts, Robert J. Seidel described Project IMPACT (Instructional Model Prototypes Attainable in Computerized Teaching) in a way that represented the dynamics and purpose

Zinn and McClintock posited for the individual-computer system. For instance, in the Zinn and McClintock collection of papers on computer developments in education, Seidel wrote:

. . . The problem for an instructional agent (human or machine) is to take optimal action in line with an overall "best" strategy for transmitting uniquely relevant information to the student. Of necessity, recurrent decisions concerning these instructional actions must be made relative to (1) the subject-matter being taught, (2) the specific student, (3) the momentary circumstances, and (4) the available options (communication channels), if specified proficiency criteria are to be attained effectively and efficiently.

. . . The total instructional system noted above is considered in Project IMPACT over four phased development cycles. The heart of this total system CAI effort is the iterative development and testing of instructional decision models (IDM's). This cyclical approach takes shape in a cybernetic system in which the set of control processes continues to be refined from the input (student data) and output (criterion performance) relationships of the successive IDM's. Within any given version, these control processes are embodied in the particular decision-making rules incorporating system experience gained up to that point.

Over the four cycles of development and testing, the four prongs of the effort (hardware, software, subject-matter and IDM) are revised and updated. The first two cycles comprise respectively the development and evaluation of the "breadboard" (preliminary) CAI system. Synthesis and implementation of the refined components into a proto-type, operational CAI system is to be undertaken in cycles three and four. (Zinn & McClintock, 1970, Appendix B, pp. 32-33)

We now have a very interesting picture in the making. Numeric analysis of educational data is becoming interactive and dynamic, by virtue of its placement in a computer environment. Instruction and educational data are, similarly, becoming interactive and dynamic by virtue of their being placed into a computer environment. The heart of this dynamic model in computer-involved education is Seidel's IDM (Instructional Decision Model), which provides a union in which numeric analysis and instruction can be thought of as a set. Interactive, dynamic, iterative thinking, and action have, thus, become both possible and feasible in education.

But why stop here? Let us venture a bit. Still another step can be taken.

13

Potential Use of ERIC System

The United States Office of Education has constructed (and re-constructed) a series of Educational Resources Information Clearinghouses (known collectively as ERIC) at various institutions. Each ERIC Clearinghouse is responsible for assembling, abstracting, indexing, and reporting the research and other literature in an assigned area. Reports are prepared by the Clearinghouse upon request. These reports may be requested by author, article, or subject. A so-called Key Word in Context indexing system (usually referred to as a KWIC system) is also in dynamic development, so that searches at levels finer than, or even different than, the original subjects indexed eventually will be accomplished with the aid of computer programs.

In summary, before taking a fourth and final step, we urge the reader to review where we have been. Such a backward look will lead one to conclude that computer programming in educational research has now developed to the point that a person can be in dynamic and interactive contact with data, for the purpose of informing oneself both explicitly and heuristically. The ERIC system permits this potential to exist in educational research in respect to research topics and subjects. Computer-aided or computer-assisted instruction permits this potential to exist in respect to instructional decision-making models (IDM's), in the union of subject and student. Finally, dynamic and interactive programming of numeric analyses creates a potential for testing specific hypothetical propositions, thus enabling one to relate educational effects to characteristics of those being educated.

We are aware that no computer system exists in which ERIC, computer-aided or computer-assisted instruction, and interactive numeric analysis are (or, even, may be) united. Such a union would be so complex that a computer system that had all of these component parts may never prove technologically feasible. In addition, economic thinking may dictate that a plan to create such a system should be one spread over a considerable amount of time, as well as one that is likely to generate a great number of potential users. For these reasons, it might seem preposterous to continue, as we will, with an argument that assumes that such a system _can_ exist. Nevertheless, we ask you to bear with us, since just such an assumption is vitally needed if students, parents, and government are to learn that multi-purposed, multi-enabling living is really possible through the aid of dynamic, powerful, interactive, and comprehensive systems of thinking and acting.

In 1969 one of us argued that a computer system _can_ be imagined that would have the specific and general effects that,

so far, we have attributed to the possible but unfeasible union
of ERIC, computer-aided instruction, and a dynamically undertaken numeric analysis (Tiedeman, 1969). However, in that argument Tiedeman did not specify the necessary design parameters
for a system of the magnitude under consideration. Furthermore, he did not integrate adequately dynamic decision making
of a second party into the self-informing, self-correcting
process one uses in making decisions. We believe we are now
ready to explore some conditions related to a good design for
inquiring into such matters.

DESIGN AND INQUIRY

We have acknowledged the necessary, logical gap between
research and education. Nevertheless, we still seek a union of
student and system that does not contradict this logical gap
but which grounds a person's future actions in both research
and thought by placing him or her directly in the system. Our
problem, as we see it, is to design a system in which the student not only may participate but also may achieve personal responsibility and control.

Many designs could be considered in specifying a relationship between a person and a set of operations that would prove
informing and, yet, would still permit one to guide action by
thought, without experiencing a threat to one's own integrity.
Which of these designs we choose makes a great difference, for
our choice will tend to determine what we can discover and how
far we can go in our understanding. For instance, in a 1955
work entitled Speculative Instruments, I. A. Richards noted the
presence of a "principle of an instrument" in both the purpose-
fulness and the endlessness of comprehension:

Through these assumptions comprehension /author's
note/ divides and combines*—dividing in order to combine,
combining in order to divide—and simultaneously. Whatever
it compares is compared in a respect or in respects. These
respects are the instruments of the exploration. And it is
with them as with the instruments of investigation in phys-
ics but more so: the properties of the instruments enter
into the account of the investigation. There is thus at
the heart of any theory or meanings a principle of the instrument. The exploration of comprehension is the task of
devising a system of instruments for comparing meanings.
But these systems, these instruments, are themselves

---

*Phaedrus, 265D-226B. I have written further on "these
processes of division and bring together" in How to Read a Page
(London: Routledge and Kegan Paul, 1943, pp. 217-222).

comparable. They belong with what they compare and are subject in the end to one another. Indeed, this mutual subjection of control seems to be the ἀρχή for a doctrine of comprehension—that upon which all else depends.*
(I. A. Richards, 1955, pp. 18-19)

Design—Ambassador

The first design that we carefully considered was that of an ambassador. In Speculative Instruments, Richards used the design of an ambassador between the realm of the humanities and the realm of science to provide further clarification of a theory of literary criticism. By thinking as if he were such an ambassador (or, perhaps, even a Commissioner of Education), Richards effectively clarified the relationship between the specific and the general that is created by a desire to be more articulate about the artistry of literature. We, too, undertake the responsibility to clarify further the relationship between the specific and the general. However, we seek a means that does not depend on someone else to clarify the relationship for a person, as an ambassador does for those he represents. We need Richard's interpretive, ambassadorial function, but we also need more than that. Our end is far more than a representation of one person's view as expressed by another; our end is personal understanding. We need means to that end. We aim for personal understanding both of another's representation of one's own views and of the subjects about which one has views.

Design—Game

The second design that we considered just as carefully involved construction of a game, particularly a game between a researcher and a student. The game we considered gave a student practice in how to ground his or her own moves in research. As we proceed in this chapter the reader will find that we use both the game design and the ambassadorial design to further our argument. However, the game design was not as satisfactory as another we identified, one which allows a person to participate in his or her own grounding of action in research.

Inquiry

Our problem is not simple. How can we approach an understanding of the mechanisms of grounding one's action in research without either posing a threat to individual freedom or failing to respect society's definition of responsibility? We will

---

*Republic, 511C. See How to Read a Page, Index: "Dependence" (London: Routledge and Kegan Paul, 1943.)

16

attempt a solution by posing the question, "Can a Machine Ground Education in Research?" By posing the question in this way, we seek understanding. We trust that the reader recognizes that we have absolutely no intention of answering the question affirmatively, at least not from the standpoint of sketching the "breadboard" of a computer system that would have the effects we seek. Our intentions are two-fold. First, we intend to start specifying conditions necessary for the eventual existence of such a system. Second, we intend to urge every citizen to live a life that is based upon a belief that such a system exists even now in the general meaning of a "system" which relates to each person's comprehension of totalities.

CAN A MACHINE GROUND EDUCATION IN RESEARCH?

The Question and Its Import

At a time when practically everyone seems to agree that only human action can be patterned, it may seem foolhardy even to ask whether a machine can ground education in research. Therefore, we agree rather quickly that we are not wondering whether something can be both human and non-human at the same time. But we are wondering if a machine can ground education in research.

Our question will fulfill our intent if the machine puts the feelings many of us have about doing research and educating into perspective. A useful question can lead to other questions. We hope to get from the question-supplied perspective a better sense of what other questions must be considered as one tries to come to terms with the idea of research-grounded education. Because of what machines are perceived to be, we think that we accomplish our task best by using the word "machine" in our question.

For instance, machines execute procedures, and each machine is the embodiment of the procedure it executes. This relationship is an important, fundamental one; it exists for all machines. Unfortunately, people are not in the habit of speaking about machines in this way. If people were, they would recognize that to know in detail what a particular machine does (i.e., to know how it works) is enough to know what procedure it is executing. The thing that counts about a machine is the way it behaves, and that behavior is prescribed by the procedure the machine executes. All automation is nothing more than the physical expression of well-formed procedures. There is no magic about it, only well-formed procedures.

When we say that a machine is the embodiment of the procedure it executes, we are maintaining that a statement of a procedure describes the machine needed to carry out that procedure. Thus, "mechanizing" means thinking about procedures, not thinking about hardware. Moreover, once we can state a procedure explicitly, we should not be surprised that a machine can be built to execute that procedure.

To make things somewhat simpler, we will confine ourselves to computers, instead of trying to consider machines in general. This restriction poses no real problem, since a computer is a device whose job is to accept descriptions of other machines and, then, to imitate their behavior in what is called a computer program. Such a program usually is thought of as a set of instructions for what the computer-machine is to do, but the program really is more than that. The program is like a blueprint that the computer uses to build itself into the particular machine needed to execute the specific procedures described by the program. The computer operates as though it were armed with pliers and screwdrivers, which the computer uses to rebuild itself to conform, step-by-step, to the procedure outlined for the computer by the program. Having done that, the computer becomes the machine that the program described and will, then, function as that machine. This remarkable feat is achieved by humans who provide the program that describes the procedures that make the process all possible.

A computer without a program will do nothing, even if it is plugged in, because computers are not like other machines. In a sense, the computer is not a machine at all (in its own right); yet, a computer can becomes many machines. In fact, a computer can become any machine which can be fully described to the computer. For example, one can build an address-printing machine, or one may write a computer program which will turn a computer into an address-printing machine. In either case, the results will be the same. However, even though both machines would be operationally equivalent, the two would differ from one another in one crucial respect: the computer can become other things, tomorrow or the next day, or whenever the program is changed.

Whereas the power of most machines rests in what they do, the power of the computer rests in what it can become. The essential idea of a computer is that it is an incomplete machine, ready to be completed in an infinite number of ways, each way producing a different machine. Thus, a computer program is, at the same time, an explicit statement of a procedure and the blueprint of a machine needed to carry out that procedure. Whether a computer can execute a given procedure depends primarily upon how well we understand the components of that procedure, and upon just how imaginative we are in conceiving procedures in terms of the basic elements of which they are comprised. Centering our attention upon a computer therefore

18

is advantageous since it requires description of a machine in terms of a statement of procedures. As a result, we are able to comprehend clearly the relationship between machines and the procedures they influence.

Imitation and Meaning

We propose to begin this portion of our analysis by considering the meaning of our question, "Can a Machine Ground Education in Research?" To do this we look first at the procedure adopted by the late Alan M. Turing in his consideration of a similar question. In 1950, Turing, an eminent English mathematician and logician, published an article entitled "Computing Machinery and Intelligence." In that article he examined the question of whether a machine can think. His first procedural step was to replace this bold question by another, "which is closely related to it and is expressed in relatively unambiguous words." Turing (1950, p. 433-434) wrote:

The new form of the problem can be described in terms of a game which we call the "imitation game." It is played with three people: a man (A), a woman (B), and an interrogator (C) who may be of either sex. The interrogator stays in a room apart from the other two. The object of the game for the interrogator is to determine which of the other two is the man and which is the woman. He knows them by labels X and Y, and at the end of the game he says either "X is A and Y is B," or "X is B and Y is A." The interrogator is allowed to put questions to A and B thus:

C: Will X please tell me the length of his or her hair? Now suppose X is actually A, then A must answer. It is A's object in the game to try to cause C to make the wrong identification. His answer might therefore be, "My hair is shingled, and the longest strands are about nine inches long."

In order that tones of voice may not help the interrogator, the answers should be written, or better still, typewritten. The ideal arrangement is to have a teleprinter communicating between the two rooms. Alternatively the question and answers can be repeated by an intermediary. The object for the third player (B) is to help the interrogator. The best strategy for her is probably to give truthful answers. She can add such things as "I am the woman, don't listen to him!" to her answers, but it will avail nothing as the man can make similar remarks.

We now ask the question, "What will happen when a machine takes the part of A in this game?" Will the interrogator decide wrongly as often when the game is played like this as he does when the game is played between a man and a woman? These questions replace our original, "Can machines think?"

Our interest in Turing's approach relates to whether or not such a procedure for establishing the meaning of a question will work for us. Can we make use of the idea of an imitation game?

Before answering that question directly, we need to point out how our consideration of educational research is already potentially different from ordinary conceptions of such research, just by virtue of thinking of the question. The possessor of knowledge of educational research is usually considered to be in an intermediate position between a student and a researcher. Assimilation of a first party's results by a third party through mediation of a second party is a central concern in everyday discussions of educational research. However, when one considers a machine for grounding education in research, one need not consider a second party at all. Both research and the resulting application of research conclusions may be imagined as co-existing in an eductional research machine. Such a machine may be conceived as educating according to the best that is known about the process, as Seidel proposed in Project IMPACT. An educational research machine that imitates the relationship between educational researcher and a student relates data and student directly, not secondarily, as we ordinarily do by first doing research and then implementing its results. We want to conceive a machine that imitates interaction between the educational researcher and the student, not interaction between the educational researcher and the teacher. We believe that the educational researcher should be the student's teacher.

Now that we have exposed a new potential by thinking about a machine instead of existing conditions, we are faced with the difficult problem of specifying the imitation that we want. Our new potential permits us to conceive of a student's direct relationship to his or her aspirations, the data and possibilities for implementation. Somewhat earlier, we proposed that interactive and dynamic relationships now can be imagined between a student and three basic sources: (a) the primary substance of teaching, via Seidel's IDM's; (b) the literature, which is the primary store of educational research; and (c) the functions of numeric analyses or existing logical means to test inferences. We want to relate a student directly with those resources so that a synergism will be created which will sustain but, also, reveal the illusion that the student is grounding his or her education in his or her research on learning. The primary relationship that must be created in constructing the needed educational research machine is one in which a student moves from decision making about his or her goals to

20

implementation. Our question has become, "What Sort of Imitative Procedure Can Have Such an Effect?"

In a paper entitled, "Can a Machine Counsel?" Ellis and Tiedeman (1970) specified two important things which a machine must be able to do: first, inform a person using it; and, second, leave that person with responsibility for determining goals and actions based on his or her own decisions. In that development, Ellis and Tiedeman rejected two forms of substitution, one of which was related to wondering, as in a "simulation," whether a machine can become the thing imitated. We choose not to bother with the question, "Can a machine be an educational researcher?", since we are convinced that it cannot. A second form of substitution, also rejected by the Ellis and Tiedeman paper, was one which Turing used in his 1950 paper, in which the imitation consisted of a machine behaving like the thing imitated. We prefer not to address the question, "Can a machine behave the way researchers do?" We choose not to put into an educational research machine the functions that educational researchers perform merely because they are human rather than because they actually inhere educationally in the research process.

Ellis and Tiedeman (1970) indicated that one gains considerably in capacity to think about the question merely by imagining that a machine can accomplish what one wants it to accomplish. They realized in their paper that when one creates a substitute machine procedure one need think only about effects on the one to be helped. One need not think of results that might relate to an intermediate party. Therefore, we now want to divest ourselves of the need to conceive of a machine as being an educational researcher, a teaching educational researcher, or even a teacher. What we seek is a machine that will have the goals, but not the beings, of all three. This attitude will permit us not to think about a machine doing what a teaching educational researcher does.

Since we seek only the effects that a student achieves from interacting with a teaching educational researcher, we need not consider the things a teaching educational researcher does merely because he is human. However, we cannot ignore the things which a machine will have to do because it is a computer to seek the ends we specify. Therefore, we must find a sense of the word "imitation" that can make possible what we seek to accomplish through interaction between a student and a machine. Aristotle described "imitation" as something more than merely copying, and we propose to base our design of a research-grounding education machine on that Aristotlean sense of the word.

21

In their earlier work, Ellis and Tiedeman, as they analyzed the question, "Can a machine counsel?", identified Aristotle's use of "imitation" in his Poetics as something different from copying. Oates and O'Neill maintained that Aristotle
"is seeking to give a secondary meaning to the term." They
suggested that Aristotle used the word to mean the process that
takes place when an artist creates his work of art. They wrote
that, "It is through mimesis (imitation) that form comes to be
imposed upon the artist's materials broadly conceived" (Oates
and O'Neill, 1938, p. xxiii). That which art imitates is nature or, more accurately, the process of nature. Thus, even
though the objects of nature are natural and the objects of art
are artificial, these objects of art "are produced as nature
would have produced them" (McKeon, 1947, p. 621). Simply
stated, art imitates nature in the processes of production, as
well as in the objects produced.

For Aristotle, the difference between art and nature
rested in the difference between an internal and an external
causation. Aristotle considered nature to be "a cause of motion internal to the thing moved, while art is an external
cause employed by the artist to impose on matter a form first
conceived in his mind" (McKeon, 1947, p. 621). This Aristote-
lian distinction is important to our purpose, because it is in
the inter-play between the internal and the external imposition
of form that we can begin to characterize our beliefs about
grounding education in research and, thus, can begin to describe the role a machine might have in such a grounding.

The artist wishes his or her audience to undergo an experience and, as a result of that experience, to become more sensitive not only to the object of the art but, even more, to the
natural phenomena which the process of its creation mirrors.
Thus, the artist differs from others not so much in ability to
draw or sculpt or to write the language gracefully, but in
ability to experience in a natural phenomenon that which others
can only experience through personal artistic expression of
that phenomenon. The artistic process--Aristotlean mimesis--is
a way of experiencing the world, and the object of such art is
communication of that experience.

We feel that Aristotle's special meaning of "imitation"
also can be used to describe, generally, the act of enlivening
research in education. We also feel that the mission of a
research-grounding machine in education can be thought of as
being much like the mission of the artist. The search for en-
lightenment from the educational researcher's material is the
student's predicament (Tiedeman, 1967). The desire, process,
and manner in which the research establishes and develops a relationship with a student, plus the subsequent creation together of the basis for a resolution of this predicament, are

22

all constituent parts of the researcher's necessary mode of "imitation." Even though few educational researchers act this way, we maintain that the enlightening researcher's intent is not merely resolution of difficulty; rather, it is revelation of the process by which resolution becomes possible. The enlightening researcher accomplishes this intent by causing form to be imposed upon a student's predicament—first, by the researcher's external representation of the process of resolution, but, eventually, through the student's insight, which results from internal experience of the process itself.

Internalization within the student is the goal of an enlightening researcher, who seeks to reach this goal by revealing through an educating relationship with students the processes of resolution in an essentially artistic way. Should the relationship itself become more important than the internalization to either student or researcher, the researcher has failed, just as a sculptor fails if the model of Man obscures the experiencing of men, the source from which the sculpture derives meaning.

What this all means, we believe, is that enlightening researchers are themselves imitators. When we wonder if a machine can ground education in research we must realize that we will confuse the issue by expecting such a machine to mimic the human researcher. Such an expectation ignores the fact that a human being is one kind of medium and a machine is another. Since machines and human beings are different media, to expect one to act like the other is much like expecting a poet quite literally to "paint" a portrait with words. One must let the machine stay a machine, but also recognize that the activity of research by human beings is a means to an end, which we would define as a condition in which the student will eventually find himself or herself. Our interest centers on the possibilities of a machine achieving this end, even though it will do so in a manner clearly different from that which human beings would use.

Now we come to the heart of our question, "Can a Machine Ground Education in Research?" We mean to ask whether it is possible to create a machine environment in which an individual who functions in certain, specified ways can be informed by the educational research functions and the results can be deliverable by the machine. We are not asking whether a machine can copy what human beings do when they do educational research. We are asking whether we can achieve an identity of goals between a researcher and a machine.

The Goals of Research in Education

Having finally settled on this interpretation for our question, and having thus gained the necessary perspective in respect to the question, we are faced with the problem of answering the question of whether a researcher and a machine can achieve goal identity. We will consider then what feat it is that a machine must accomplish (Note: We do not say, "what a machine must do") for the answer to be a definite "Yes." For the moment, the primary concern must be with the basis on which the question is to be answered. Following satisfaction of that concern, then we can assess the possibilities that such a machine can exist.

Because we posed the question to gain perspective on our beliefs about what research-grounded education is, we will now present those beliefs in a general form, although we speak about a particular concept of research in education. We believe that both the way the problem is viewed and the approach to its solution are general in nature. We recognize the diversity that can be tolerated within this general approach. However, we offer one notion of research in education, not so much to argue its merits as to provide a case in point, from which we propose to evolve a basis for an answer to our question in its present form.

As we understand them, the ultimate goals in science consist of becoming both more explicit and more credible about what one claims scientifically. These ultimate goals of science can never be realized fully, because no one can ever be completely explicit about what one thinks and because credibility is always being sought, never fully achieved. Furthermore, the forms of communication (that realm in which explicitness and credibility co-exist) are themselves never co-extensive with the forms of thought of the scientist or, for that matter, with those with whom the scientist seeks to communicate.

Although the scientist knows that ultimate goals are unattainable, the individual accepts the obligation to work toward them. That obligation means, in turn, that the processes by which thought and explanation interact are critical in understanding what it means to be "doing science." This interaction of thought and explanation constitutes the principal subject matter of any consideration of "method" in science. Therefore, we shall address ourselves to the interaction of thought and explanation, because (as we hinted earlier) designing an educating research machine paradoxically offers new potential: it offers a way to expand the power of what we have formerly done and it gives us a new means of posing an ever-continuing interest in method.

Because goals of education researchers are always being pursued, but never fully achieved, we assert that such researchers must deal with their problems as examples of Aristotle's artistic imitation (mimesis). Researchers can deal with these problems by concerning themselves and their students with the processes by which such problems in general may be resolved. In this way, some specific problem and the resultant condition in which it leaves the student may be used by the researcher as the material with which to fashion an understanding of the process of problem-forming and problem-solving. For this reason, simply giving information or advice, even "good" advice, is not enough, by itself, to result in grounding education in research.

Problem and Understanding. To be more specific, one should expect students to ground their education in research when they have "problems" related to their understandings.* The words "understanding" and "problem" are not completely satisfactory choices in the context of our meaning since, in ordinary language, they do not convey all that is intended. For instance, "understanding" usually is used in a far too limited way, while "problem" is usually used in a far too general way to suit our exact needs. Nonetheless, these words contain the requisite grains of meaning we seek.

By the word "understanding" we do not mean just a person's recall skill, knowledge, or even appreciation, although each is part of our meaning. We want to expand the word's meaning, and we want to change its frame of reference. However, we do not want to suggest that "understanding" is something that is pieced together, or definable by whatever may be included in its set of meanings. Understanding is not definable solely in terms of its constituent meanings anymore than movement in a motion picture is definable in terms of the frames that make up the film, or anymore than an electrical current can be defined solely in terms of the piecing together of electrons. Motion and flow are not inherent in the objects that move or the liquids that flow; rather, they are the impressions that moving and flowing things leave upon the beholder. Thus, while motion may be inferred from objects that move, it is not (in the strictest sense) made up of those objects. We perceive understanding in these terms.

---

*We use the strong word "problem" here, even though we consider that a problem is not the only thing that can be an appropriate motivation for seeking educational research. Curiosity, for example, may well be equally appropriate, as may the involvement of a game-playing maze.

We view understanding _per se_ as the time-extended "working out" or articulation of a self in a problem situation. Thus, we depart from a mere behavioral meaning of "understanding" and place it in the context of individual purposes and problems. Thus, the artistry required of the enlivening educational researcher, as we conceive it, consists in revealing to the student the _nature_ of the understandings inherent in his or her purposes. Articulation of a self in a problem provides the context and the opportunity for "expression of hope and desire and limitation upon life" (Tiedeman and O'Hara, 1963, p. iv). By the working out of a self in a problem the continuity that we would call understanding is created. While purposive behavior is central to the process, we do not consider understanding, strictly speaking, to be a road that _leads_ somewhere. Instead, understanding is a "trace" resembling the bread trail left by Hansel and Gretel. For us, understanding is the _consequence_ of _passage_.

Deciding. The mechanism for the working out of a self in a problem, and thus for inscription of understanding, is the activity of deciding. This contention leads to the defining of the word "problem" as a situation involving some difficulty with deciding. Deciding is so important to the process, as we see it, because the exercise of individual freedom, through choice, is what makes understanding become a time-extended mapping of a self in a problem, instead of just a temporary smoke or bread trail.

One difficulty a person might have with deciding could arise from lack of ability to be decisive: the person simply may not know how to decide. Another difficulty could arise from being unaware of the nature of the decision. Perhaps the most general difficulty a person can have with deciding, however, arises from an inadequate sense that one _can_ decide. (This difficulty is what most desperately needs the presence and action of an enlivening educational researcher.) Absence of a clear sense that one _can_ be an agent in determining what happens in one's education and in one's life is at the base of much of the trouble people have with deciding.

A Sense of Agency. Ultimately the most important educational task of all is to accomplish a transfer from "helper" to "student" of control over events; or, as Field (1970) said, make a switch in "navigational systems." From birth, throughout infancy and much of childhood, and until some unspecifiable point in an individual's development, each person's interactions with his or her environment are guided primarily by external controls. Whether it be all at once, or through a bit by bit process, some societies utilize systematic procedures to provide individuals at least partial acceptance of responsibility for control of their own lives. In our democratic society we believe that the educational process has the basic task of transferring the "navigational systems" from a primarily external to a primarily internal control. We use the term to define individual capacity or responsibility for control over one's own life. By extension, we use a sense of agency* to express the belief, the trust, the faith that one does, in fact, possess such a personal capacity or responsibility.

Specifics of the process of decision making in which a sense of agency is engendered may be characterized by a paradigm proposed by Tiedeman and O'Hara (1963). In confining that paradigm to the rational form of decision making, Tiedeman and O'Hara stated that, "It seems sufficient to suggest a paradigm of the process of reaching a rational decision since such is the differentiated and later integrated condition that the practices of /research/ attempt to facilitate." (Tiedeman and O'Hara, 1963, p. 38) Through the notion of decision making, as depicted in that paradigm, we will view the researcher's effort to impose form on the student's predicament and, thereby, reveal the processes by which the imposition of such form can be achieved.

The Process of Decision Making. According to the Tiedeman and O'Hara paradigm, the process of decision making is divided into two aspects that are termed anticipation and accommodation. The anticipation aspect of decision making consists of a person's preoccupation with two kinds of things: first, the pieces (e.g., the facts, alternatives, options, and consequences) out of which a decision is to be fashioned, and, second, the affective context (e.g., the aspirations, hopes, expectations, constraints and the like) which will determine the form of the decision. The accommodation aspect (also called "the aspect of implementation or adjustment") of decision making represents movement from anticipation to induction. It is the point in the decision-making process where imagination meets reality.

Tiedeman and O'Hara's general paradigm for decision making included a series of "sub-aspects" or "stages" within both anticipation and accommodation. Their paradigm identified four stages within the anticipatory aspect and three stages for the accommodative aspect.

_____

*This concept bears some resemblance to, but is not specifically derived from "fate control," as documented by Coleman (1966) and the model of "competence" developed by White (1959). The theory of purposeful action in which the concept of "agency" is founded has been reported by Field (1970).

The first stage of the <u>anticipation</u> aspect of decision making was termed one of <u>exploration</u> by Tiedeman and O'Hara. This stage begins, they asserted, with a person's awareness "that a problem does or will exist and that a decision must be reached in order to resolve it in a satisfying manner" (1963, p. 38). They also discussed this first stage of exploration in the following way:

> In the step of exploration . . . a number of different alternatives or possible goals . . . may be considered. Relevant goals are those which can possibly be attained from the opportunities associated with the problem under consideration. . . . During the exploratory step fields are relatively transitory, highly imaginary (perhaps even fantastic), and not necessarily related one to the other. They may be a relatively unassociated set of possibilities and consequences. . . . In the step of exploration in relation to a problem of growing understanding, a person probably reflects at least upon his aspiration, opportunity both now and in the future, interest, capability, distasteful requirements that still can be tolerated, and societal context for himself and his dependents. These are relevant aspects of the field set by each goal. In short, a person attempts to take the measure of himself /and his understandings/ in relation to each alternative as he senses it. (1963, pp. 38 & 41)

Tiedeman and O'Hara gave the name <u>crystallization</u> to the second stage of the <u>anticipation</u> aspect. Of it they asserted the following:

> In /crystallization/ the cost of the several goals can be considered in relation to the return from each. The value of alternatives can then be assessed. Relevant considerations are organized or ordered in this process of valuing. . . . The process of valuing gives rise to values which tend to fix the organization or order of all relevant considerations in relation to each of the goals as crystallization occurs. . . . Crystallization normally represents a stabilization of thought. A setting of thought is achieved which is ordinarily of some durability and hence of some reliance. This set readies the person for investment of self along a line that then becomes more noticeable. The situation becomes defined, so to speak, at least for a time. (1963, p. 41)

<u>Choice</u> was the name given to the third stage of the <u>anticipation</u> aspect of decision making. In the paradigm, this stage follows readily upon that of crystallization. Tiedeman and O'Hara wrote the following of this third stage:

28

With choice, a particular goal, and its relevant field
. . . orients the behavioral system of the person to relevance for his problem. . . . This goal may be elected with
varying degrees of certainty and its motive power will vary
as a result. . . . Furthermore, the degrees of clarity,
complexity, and freedom generally available to the person
in the solution of this problem and in the pursuit of the
indicated decision will also affect the motivating power of
the resulting resolution of alternatives. (1963, p. 42)

Tiedeman and O'Hara posited a fourth and final stage of the
anticipation aspect, which they called clarification. Although
one might expect, once a choice had been made, that aspects of
decision making that precede action would be completed, this is
not necessarily so. Though a decision is made and even firmly
held, doubt often arises. Thus, they posited that it is true:

. . . in even a short period of waiting (a week or
more, say) for the expected situation to begin to unfold
. . . doubt experienced in the waiting period causes the
individual further to clarify his anticipated position. An
elaboration and perfection of the image of the future . . .
ensues. . . . Clarification not only perfects the image of
self in position, but also dissipates some of the former
doubts concerning the decision. (1963, p. 43)

In their 1963 paradigm, Tiedeman and O'Hara allowed for
three stages during the accommodation aspect of decision making. These three stages they called induction, reformation,
and integration. They described each of these stages in the
following way:

1. The stage of Induction:

A general defense of self and a giving up of an aspect
of self to group purpose /and understanding/; . . . the individual's goal and field assimilatively become a part of
the region . . . of the social system in which the person
is implementing his desired solution of his problem. He
learns the premises and structures-in-interaction required
for continued identification. This process leads to a further perfection of individual goal and field in the social
system. . . . (1963, p. 44)

2. The stage of Reformation:

The receptive orientation of induction /gives7 . . .
way to /an7 assertive orientation. . . . The person is
well immersed in a relevant group /and its required under-
standings7. . . . He has a strong sense of self and actively enjoins the group to do better. . . . Since . . .

29

the person acts both upon the in-group goal and field . . .
in order to bring that group into greater conformance with
his modified goal and field . . . and upon the out-group to
bring their view of his identification into greater con-
sistency with his, the effect, if any, is the modification
of group goal and field. . . . (1963, p. 44)

3. The stage of Integration:

Synthesis is, of course, the essence of integration.
. . . A differentiation in identification has been achieved.
The new-found appreciation of self is integrated with its
larger field. This new part of the self-system becomes a
working member of the whole self-system. In integration,
individual and group both strive to keep the resulting organization of collaborative activity. . . . The individual
is satisfied, at least temporarily, when integration occurs. (1963, p. 44)

This particular paradigm of the decision-making process
contains a potential difficulty that is quite similar to one we
sometimes face as we use language. For some time, philosophers
have considered the peculiar problem resulting from the fact
that language is used to talk about language itself. For example, Bertrand Russel has shown that a bad "philosophical syntax"
is to assert something like "The golden mountain does not exist" and, from that, suppose one is attributing some kind of
existence to the very thing whose existence is denied by the
sentence. As language sometimes does, the paradigm of decision
making turns back onto itself in a way that we must understand.

Not only does the Tiedeman and O'Hara paradigm depict the
decision-making process but, by this very depiction, it pre-
scribes how one should relate to that process. In the aspect
of accommodation, the paradigm argues that one of the things
which one must "accommodate" is the decision-making process itself. However, integration or comprehension is the development of meaning, meaning that is independent of the language
through which it is expressed. Thus, the language of decision
making, even though it is the inescapable medium through which
understanding of the process comes, must be "thrown off" before
the "accommodation" is really complete.

This "throwing off" (or, perhaps even better, this making
invisible) of the instrument of meaning gets us back to the Aristotlean play between the external and the internal imposition
of form. Accommodation to decision making is very general in
nature, since it represents an internalization of the processes
of resolution. First, the language must be established for an
individual (i.e., via induction). Then, the language itself
must become an object of analysis (i.e., via reformation).

Finally, the language must dissolve, as an individual goes past it to meaning (i.e., via integration or comprehension).

The enlivening researcher must take a student through these phases or "stages," not so much with respect to a particular problem as to the process itself. The researcher must establish within the student a proficiency in the language of the process and an awareness of this language and its effects before internalization of the process can be accomplished. In doing this, we argue that a logical consequence is that the researcher leaves a student with an important gift, a sense of agency. We argue, further, that the conviction that one is a significant agent in determining what happens to oneself does not come from convincing a person that this is so, but from internalization of the decision-making process.

Three Requirements of a Machine. Having presented a brief explanation of our views of research, we can now pursue the terms under which an answer to our basic question might be formulated. Before we could say that a person had been educated by a research machine, that machine would have to have accomplished at least three things. First, it would have to have reflected the elements of decision making in such a way that the language of the research process was exposed to the person. (Naturally, this exposure to the language of the research process must have developed a proficiency in its use.) Second, the machine must have encouraged a person to develop an awareness of the process and, as well, the relation of a self to a problem as viewed by that process. (That is, the research process must have become a mechanism for manipulating the relationship between a self and a predicament.) Third, and finally, the machine must have allowed and fostered a person's accommodation to the decision-making process in terms of both a specific predicament and, even more importantly, the process in general. Because we seek only an identity of goals between a machine and an educational researcher, we need not expect the "act" of educational research to be carried out in the same way by a machine and a human researcher. If we can achieve an identity of goals and have an assurance that the goals can be accomplished, then we would be willing to say that a person could be educated by a research machine.

Design of an Information System for Educational
Decision Making: An Example of an ISED

We already have admitted that an educating research machine is not likely to exist. The sheer magnitude and awesome complexity of the necessary system would, we very strongly suspect, boggle our present generation of computer programmers and system analysts and, quite possibly, overtax even our largest computer facilities. We also strongly suspect that the

31

magnitude and complexity of the system would frighten those with the funds to finance it, for they would have to let us play with their monies. Under these conditions, it may seem absurd to push our argument any further than we have already. However, we are engaged in an exercise that, to us, is not absurd at all. We have already argued that the rudiments of an educating research machine exist right now. We can conceive of designing the student into the educating research machine system without either threatening his or her freedom or depriving those necessary "others" of their right and obligation to set levels of expectation. Moreover, in the immediately previous section of this chapter we established the design conditions that, in our view, must be maintained for freedom to exist in the face of expectation.

The primary concern is creation of an infrastructure which, in its artistry, will inform the responsible judgement of a student, who could never really be deprived of responsibility for self-education and self-correction, even through overt violence and coercion. The heart of such an infrastructure is the way it helps a student go about decision making, especially when one presumes that a student follows his or her own desires while seeking personal satisfactions.

From 1966 through 1970, several colleagues worked with one of us to create what Seidel would call the "breadboard" of an Information System for Vocational Decisions (ISVD).* The heart of that ISVD consisted of individual participation of students in a system that was designed to have the effects we have prescribed for an educating research machine. We can therefore take a further step toward an outline of the personal decision-making position in a person-computer interaction. As we take this further step we will be torn constantly between whether to leave the existing example of a decision-making system (ISVD) within the vocational realm where it now works, or to extend it for young people to include educational decision making. In our view, research grounded decision making in education can exist in young people, if not in a machine, provided they develop their own capacities to discern the processes of thought-informed action in any realm of purpose.

Distinction Between Data and Information. Simon (1969) established a potentially useful distinction between what he termed data (i.e., facts) and information (i.e., facts interpreted in relation to use) as he considered the design issues

---

*The Principal Investigators in the ISVD project were Gil Boyer, Russell Davis, Richard Durstine, Allan Ellis, Wallace Fletcher, Edward Landy, Robert O'Hara, David Tiedeman, and Michael Wilson.

in the artificial sciences. We believe that the underlying
theory supporting our proposed Information System for Educational Decisions (ISED) also must be oriented by this distinction between data and information. The task of the educational
information system must be essentially that of enabling the individual to transform data into information.

Transformation of data into information is, we think, to
be achieved by teaching the individual to interpret data in
light of his or her own knowledge, experience, and intention.
This personal relationship to data will result in their individualized organization and use in the process of decision making. We presume that only when data are used in this way can
they be described accurately as information, at least as far as
the individual is concerned. Information that is so generated
can however then serve as data when making future decisions.
The quality of decisions is directly related to kind, quality,
and comprehensiveness of data transformed into information by
an individual during the process of decision making. Therefore,
a fundamental task of research in education is to identify,
evaluate, and classify needed data and, then, to make data
readily available to students in usable forms at times when
they need data and in places where they require data.

Throughout passage from point to point in the decision-
making process associated with one's expansion of intelligence,
one continues to turn data into information. This observation
must be a major concern of an ISED, since, in the real world,
data are never complete, and neither is information. This incompleteness is precisely what often makes a decision necessary.
In any event, quality of the choice or decision depends upon
quality of the data available. Therefore, before one attempts
to make a decision, one first must understand the "incompleteness" of the data and information with which one is dealing.

Accepting data and information on these terms leads rather
naturally to a condition or state in which one is more likely
to take responsibility for choices made, since they are not
"choices" that are totally determined by external, controlling
factors. If one's "choices" were so controlled, then "choice"
would be either irrelevant or superfluous since defensible alternatives would not exist. Moreover, to create information
out of data upon which one can base a decision, one must process data actively, rather than be guided passively by them.
Therefore, the individual must become a significant agent in
the whole choice process.

Incompleteness of data implies that an individual is responsible for decisions (i.e., the "responsibility" cannot be
allocated to someone or something external to oneself). Only
an individual makes decisions, and only such an individual

33

either enjoys or suffers the consequences. This is one way to define "freedom," and it is to this notion of "freedom" that we believe an ISED must be dedicated. An ISED will achieve our goal by developing in the student the ability to engage in just this kind of decision making relative to his or her own understandings. Specifically, the system we conceive would place a student among resources, enhance access to them, teach the stages in decision making and, then, have him or her engage the resources in a controlled setting, so that skills for processing data into information and for making informationally relevant decisions could develop.

Monitoring. An additional factor in the decision-making procedure we envisage for our proposed ISED is what we term monitoring. Monitoring consists of keeping track of the student as he or she goes repeatedly from stage to stage through the decision-making paradigm. Aside from the usual reasons for monitoring a student's behavior (e.g., to analyze performance, to select from alternate courses of action, or just generally to maintain an account of the student's interaction with the system), our proposed ISED monitors so that it can present the student with results of the monitoring. This permits the student to use those results as additional data to be processed into further information. This would create a kind of meta-data, which the student would process simultaneously with other data. (We find the idea of data and meta-data to be analogous to the philosophical notions of being and becoming.)

Pattern of Action. Not only would an individual act in our proposed ISED but, more importantly, he or she would become aware of a pattern of action. The result desired from such a procedure is a higher order of understanding that includes both the decision-making act and the whole panorama of substantive choices which link points in the decision-making process. Subject-matter understanding, thus, becomes a time-extended set of choices, and, at any given point, decision making is enhanced by an over-all awareness of the road being travelled.

Feedback and Feedforward. Our ISED System proposes a model of decision-making behavior capable of providing both "feedback back" and "feedforward," to use Richards' term (Richards, 1968). It is, of course, the individual's own "feedforward" that is important. The system provides an interactive setting in which an individual engages one or more data files in certain specifiable ways, first to determine alternatives and, then, to select from among them on the basis of his or her own understandings.

Reckoning Environment. We seek a setting that will develop in the student an ability to engage in the decision-making process which we described earlier as the Tiedeman and O'Hara paradigm. We shall call such a setting a reckoning environment, because we want a student to do more than just make up his or her mind. We want that student to figure up, measure, estimate, judge, make calculated guesses and, in the end, both decide and take responsibility for the decision. This is, of course, what "deciding" actually means, but all too often people equate decision making with what we would term choice making and, thereby, miss the inherent notion of the process and its extension over time. When that happens, what is usually left is the mistaken idea that a person decides by "making up his mind." Thus, we hear about the so-called moment of decision, as if it all happened at a point in time that is discrete and unaffected by either thought or reflection. It is precisely this misconception, and the resulting inflexibility, that we challenge in our proposed ISED by calling the setting for educational decision making that we are creating an educational reckoning environment.

Once one recognizes that data and information are never "complete," it becomes wise and, even vital, to require that choice be made with the "best" possible available data. One must ask four important questions about data: Are they accurate? How complete are they? Do they fully reflect the complexity with which one must deal? Can one get them in time to explore alternatives adequately? When one asks these questions, it becomes apparent that a library by itself is unsatisfactory as a source of data, because the time involved in searching is often more than an individual can afford. Large amounts of data (e.g., descriptions of objects) can be stored, indexed, cross-referenced and, generally, made available in a library, but that is only part of what is needed. In contrast, a computer is capable of all of this, and of providing fast access as well, so that excessive search time need not delay decision making. Moreover, a computer can interact with a user-student and, thereby, help in asking relevant questions about the subject he or she is attempting to assimilate and use. Therefore, our proposed ISED looks to the computer as a device to store large amounts of data and, upon request, to make them immediately and selectively available to an individual proceeding through the decision-making process. Given that kind of accessibility, an individual can merge with the resources and become more integrated into the educational reckoning environment. As a consequence, available data become more and more like extensions of the self and less and less like "external" qualities; that is, they move toward becoming information for the individual.

In addition to a student, two other components exist within our proposed ISED reckoning environment. The first of these is an extensive collection of data about the objects and conceptions of language, the humanities, and the sciences.

Facts about linguistics, history, the social sciences, the natural sciences, and about the individual student are types of data to be stored, organized into major data files, and made available to the student as user. Each of these major data files would be separate from the others, but would be cross-referenced with them (whenever possible), so that a student-user could follow a question through several of its aspects.

Between a student-user and such major data files we propose to place a research-grounding education machine which is diagrammed in Figure 1.1. The function we envision for this final component of the ISED reckoning environment would be to facilitate a student's access to data and vice versa. We wish not only to provide a means for a student to gain convenient access to data but also to keep track of his or her access to that data. Consequently, not only can an individual get facts with which to make decisions but, just as importantly, he or she can also gain a sense of the way _he_ or _she_ goes about making a decision.

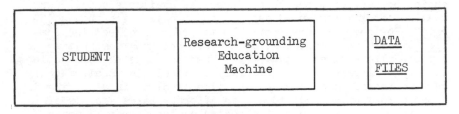

Figure 1.1. A diagram of an ISED reckoning environment.

For the rest of this chapter we will refer to our proposed machine as a "research-grounding education machine." We posit its placement as a facilitating intermediary between the student-user and the data files. Our purpose has been to create a sufficiently explicit description of the behavior of a research-grounding education machine so that a computer could be instructed to behave as if it were such a machine. Our further efforts to create such a description tend to fall into two categories, the first of which is development of the software necessary for the over-all system. This software would consist of fairly elaborate computer programs that permit basic, generally required functions to be performed. (In point of fact, the set of computer programs would probably be almost preposterously large and, we suspect, have a relatively low probability of existing within the foreseeable future.) The ISED reckoning environment must operate in a time-shared setting, so that more than one student can use the system at any one time. Furthermore, the system must provide the user (and itself) with the ability to create, maintain, edit, and retrieve data files. In addition, a programming language must exist that allows both strong manipulation and list processing. Programs are needed for statistical analyses to be readily available in the system, as well as routines that permit content analysis. In general, the system also must be able to keep track of who is on the system and what needs to be done next. This is the kind of software needed by our ISED reckoning environment, including our research-grounding education machine.

The second category of our concern involves development of specific ISED software. In some ways, this category is the more interesting one, for it relates directly to our effort to create belief that a _person_ (_homo sapiens_) can be a research-grounding education machine, although a computer may never be one. This category of software concerns the ability of our conceptualized time-shared computer to behave like a research-grounding education machine that is most likely to generate substantive contributions.

In Figure 1.2 the diagram depicts, in a quite general and incomplete way, the over-all organization we imagine for the software in an ISED reckoning environment. This diagram is based on the plan for an operating Information System for Vocational Decisions (ISVD), which we offer as a general design for what we are conceiving as an Information System for Educational Decisions (ISED). The ISED/ISVD software may be divided into four parts, each of which plays a role in development of the student-user's sensitivity to the decision-making process and moves him or her toward its internalization.

Types of Resources. Before examining the ISED/ISVD model in detail, recall what we have already said in earlier portions of this chapter about presently available resources for an interactive, dynamic educational research activity. We identified Seidel's Instructional Decision Model (i.e., the IDM) as Richards' so-called "principle of the instrument." We want an ISED reckoning environment which offers _each_ student-user sufficient access to the structure of every IDM which moves him or her into later aspects of the decision-making model we have taken from Tiedeman and O'Hara (1963). To do this, we believe that three types of resources must be available to the student who operates in the ISED reckoning environment.

The first type of resource that must be available to the student-user is the _file of basic data_ about the objects and the concepts of a subject, particularly a subject which the student-user is attempting to assimilate. We see this as involving Seidel's IDM concept and its related programming.

The second type of resource that must be made available to a student is the _literature_ dealing specifically with

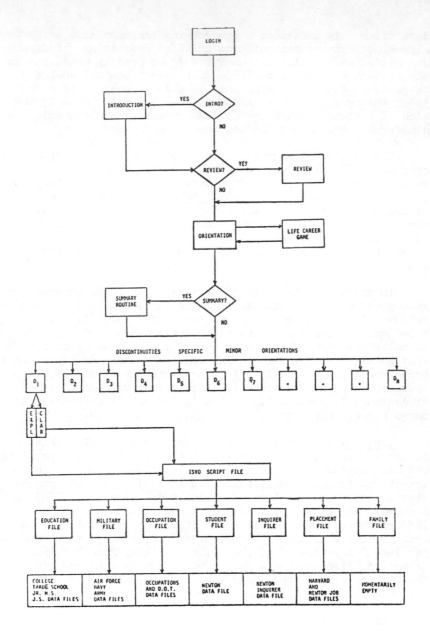

Figure 1.2. A diagramatic overview of an Information System for Vocational Decisions (ISVD) as an example of an Information System for Educational Decisions (ISED).

assimilation of the chosen subject. We see this as involving
something akin to an interactive ERIC potential.

The third type of resource that the student needs to have
available must consist of the functions of research that permit
a person to do three things: (a) assemble data, (b) identify
general concepts to be applied when selecting examples from
among available data, and (c) subordinate chosen data within a
more superordinate and, therefore, simpler structure, which
then becomes the student's theory of that detail. This last
function of the research activity—subordinate chosen data—we
suspect involves an interactive, logical analysis.

In Figure 1.2 the over-all organization of the operating
ISVD software is displayed. This system illustrates the types
of design and design problems that one will encounter when attempting to consolidate the three types of resources for an
ISED reckoning environment into a decision-making, but person-
freeing, form of imitation (Aristotlean mimesis) which ISVD was
intended to be. We believe we will learn much by contrasting
the ISVD with the ISED that is still in a state of development.

Software Components. The software in the ISVD may be divided into four parts, each of which plays a role in the
student-user's development of an understanding of the decision-
making process which grounds his or her education in research.
Of course, within the ISVD environment this research has to do
with careers, a limited aspect of the student-user's total,
over-all education.

The first of these four parts consists of the ISVD data
files. In Figure 1.2 these data files are represented in the
bottom two rows. To date, thirteen such data files are included in the ISVD. The original plan called for the number of
such data files to be increased as time passed. However, even
though the thirteen data files that exist in the ISVD environment are different from one another in a number of respects,
all of them have an essentially similar over-all structure.
Therefore, we believe that the following brief description of
one of those data files will both indicate what all of the data
files are like and suggest what a data file would have to be
like in an ISED reckoning environment.

The ISVD Occupations Data File: An Example

The ISVD occupations data file contains about fifty (50)
facts on each of about eight hundred fifty (850) different occupations. These facts relate to such things as wages, educational prerequisites, physical demands, worker traits, high
school courses needed and the like. The fifty or so facts
about each occupation are grouped together to form an

occupational _record_. In the ISVD these are called level-zero records, with one being provided for each of the eight hundred fifty occupations in the ISVD occupational data file.

In addition to these level-zero records, provision is made for including hierarchical records—records at level-one, level-two, level-three and so forth—which could be thought of as _summary records_. The level-one records in the occupational data file are used in the ISVD to represent, simultaneously, many different _logical_ organizations of the data, without concern for their physical organization. One set of such level-one records might be used to characterize the level-zero records in terms of Roe categories (Roe, 1956), while another set might represent someone else's occupational taxonomy.

Besides these two kinds of records, the ISVD occupational data file contains a fairly extensive collection of incomplete (but completeable) English sentences. These template sentences are expressed generally in such forms as: "The salary of X is Y," or "To be an X requires Y years of education." If a student-user of the ISVD should ask something like, "How much do doctors earn?" or "How long do I have to go to school to become a plumber?", then the variables X and Y in the template sentences would be replaced by the appropriate words or facts and results would be presented to the student-user. Use of such template sentences, or even of template paragraphs, need not be as seemingly trivial as the examples. However, to program for the acceptance (understanding) of natural language, so that a "conversation" in thoroughly "natural" language is possible, is no simple matter. Numerous programmers can attest to this fact.

The present, existing version of the ISVD environment contains in its thirteen initial data files several _million_ items of data, each potentially relevant to a career choice by a student-user. This part of the ISVD software is, by no means, complete. Still, it is sufficiently extensive to allow us to use it for a non-trivial exploration.

The second of the four parts of the ISVD software consists of a _network_ of _routines_ that are called _scripts_. In many ways, these scripts are the most significant components of the ISVD software. A _script_ is not unlike the manuscript of a play (indeed, it is that analog that gave these routines their name), for a _script_ is a set of rules that describes how the ISVD guidance machine is to act. Scripts contain such things as the text to be presented to a student (via either a video display device or a printer), commands to activate a device (a tape recorder, a motion picture projector, or a slide projector to show a single 35 mm. slide), instructions for processing the student-user's responses, and rules regarding computation, storage or retrieval of data.

Some scripts deal with concepts underlying the decision-making process. These are termed "teaching scripts." Superficially, these teaching scripts resemble the usual computer-aided instruction material, in which inquirer control is small compared to system control. A second kind of concept script is termed a preference script. Preference scripts are used to assist a student-user in considering the factors upon which a choice might be based. A preference script (in the ISVD environment) processes the associated data file, leaving behind only records that conformed to the stated preference. A third kind of concept script is termed a direct-access script. Such a script is used to retrieve specific bits of data from the data files.

The third part of the four parts of the ISVD software consists of three Access Routines, EXPLORATION, CLARIFICATION and REVIEW. These three access routines engage a student-user in behavior representative of the Tiedeman and O'Hara decision paradigm (as outlined in an earlier portion of this chapter). These routines are used within the ISVD environment as if they were filters between a student-user and his or her access to the data files. They are intended to develop the student-user's proficiency in, and awareness of, the decision-making process per se. It would seem that in such access routines must rest the artistry that is inherent in the function of counseling. (An example of how these three Access Routines actually operate can be found in the ISVD Project's Second Annual Report and Third Report (Tiedeman, 1969b, 1970)).

The fourth of the four parts of the ISVD software consists of a series of other routines that form the backdrop of the whole ISVD environment. These routines perform the important task of getting the student-user to the appropriate place in the ISVD. When, for instance, a student-user "logs on" to the ISVD, he or she is given an introduction, should one be needed. Then the student is asked what he or she wishes to do. These backdrop routines process the student-user's answer and determine the "career discontinuity" with which he or she is dealing. (These so-called "career discontinuities" are represented in Diagram 2 of the blocks labeled D_1, D_2, etc., and appear in a row about midway between the top and bottom of the diagram.) Then another background routine determines whether the student-user is in a phase of "exploration" or "clarification" with respect to this particular career discontinuity. Once this phase has been determined, the student-user is "passed through" to the most appropriate access routine. From that point, the student-user will be provided access to scripts which are relevant to the situation. These scripts will, in turn, provide

the student-user with access to the data files which contain
the basic data in the ISVD environment.

Three Requirements of a Machine. This description of a
student-user's passage through the ISVD environment from "log
on" to access to the data files is, obviously, an oversimplifi-
cation. But it makes an important point, since it demonstrates
just how this ISVD environment works as a functioning guidance
machine. Specifically, it indicates how (through scripts) the
student-user's proficiency with the elements of decision making
is developed and how (through access routines) the student-
user's awareness of the process underlying those elements is
progressively developed. These achievements are, as we noted
earlier, two of the three things that either a machine or a human being must accomplish to ground education properly in research. The first of these criteria was that the machine-
person interaction would have to reflect the elements of
decision-making about a self in an education problem in such a
way that the language of the process was exposed to the person.
The second of these criteria was that the machine must encourage development of an awareness of the decision-making process
in a person, especially the articulation of decisions and the
relation of a self to a problem. The third and final criterion
was that the machine must allow for and foster a person's accommodation to the decision-making process, in terms both of a
specific predicament and (even more importantly) of the process
in general. This third achievement is what we believe to be
the heart of the whole matter.

In development of the first prototype of the ISVD environment, this third requirement for a machine that could ground
education in research received the least attention. Clearly,
it was the most difficult issue the ISVD developers faced and,
although the developers had certain hunches, they were nowhere
near as clear as we would like to be now, especially as we conceive of an ISED reckoning environment. One hunch of the ISVD
developers concerned the monitoring function. It was similar
to what we have described as our vision of how to monitor
student-user interaction with the system to reveal to that
student-user the process used and his or her relation to it.

Another of the developers' hunches about this third requirement of a research-grounding education machine concerned
the games they adopted for use in the ISVD environment. The
Life Career Game developed by Sarane Boocock (1967), for instance, was one of several included (or considered includable)
in ISVD by its developers. This game allows a person to develop and go through a whole life plan for any number of ficti-
tious persons. Through use of the Life Career Game, the ISVD
developers hoped to have a student-user experience some of the
more realistic concomitants of personal choice. They placed

the game where they did in the ISVD environment (see Figure 1.2) to indicate that it is a part of, not merely a component of, the ISVD. The Life Career Game was perceived as a "point of view" about the total system, the ISVD environment. The developers felt that it allowed the student-user to function within the ISVD environment either with his or her own, real interests or with those of someone he or she pretended to be. Either orientation to use of the ISVD seemed valuable for a student-user.

Developers of the ISVD environment believed that the Boocock game provided two major advantages. First, it provided objectivity by allowing one to deal with someone else's predicaments. Second, it provided the student-user playing the game with the extension in time or the extensive series of events that normally comes only to a person through actual experience. However, these advantages were viewed only as probabilities, for the ISVD environment has not been used enough to allow one to validate hunches through accumulated experience.

Command Language. Although the command language used in the ISVD made only a small contribution to accommodation to the system, it did reflect the decision-making process built into the ISVD environment. With this relatively simple command language, a student-user could take over control of the system flow, moving about within it in the way he or she wished. Such behavior, the developers felt, would be very similar to that characteristic of the integration stage of the accommodation aspect of the decision-making process. Therefore, the developers felt able to project a possibility that one could accommodate to a machine-based system and, thereby, to the processes embodied by that system.

We recognize that this imaginative possibility may be slightly overstated. We also recognize that we would be forced to qualify that overstatement more than we wish to do if we intended to argue that the ISVD's "guidance machine" could actually counsel, or that our envisioned ISED environment and its research-grounding education machine, could really educate on its own. However, it is not our intention to push our argument quite that far.

Reprise: Can a Machine Ground Education in Research?
The Argument Restated

In this chapter we have examined one single question: Can a Machine Ground Education in Research? At this point, we want to reiterate our position, which is that the question must be answered negatively. A "machine" cannot ground education in research. In fact, as the reader should be aware by now, we cannot even specify completely the procedures necessary to create such a research-grounding education machine. We are forced to conclude, therefore, that only two courses are available presently. We can continue the present practice, in which an educational researcher investigates education alone, but we do not prefer this possibility. On the other hand, we _could_ educate students to _live_ as researchers who would research their own education. We much prefer this possibility, and have argued at length to persuade the reader that it is a real, viable and preferable alternative.

We suggested that the functions an ISED environment would have to fulfill for a student-user included substance, informing, accommodation and ease. Our hypothetical ISED environment would need to include a substance (analogous to the ISVD data files). It would need to include the capacity for a student-user to query and use the substance to inform his or her own percepts (analogous to the function of the ISVD scripts). It would also need to insure, as a result of querying a substance for the purposes of informing onself, that accommodation to the decision-making process in that substance occurred (analogous to the function of the ISVD access routines). Finally, it would need to provide the student-user of the ISED environment an effortless ease of movement, or freedom, within the ISED environment itself (analogous to the ISVD background programming). Through our efforts to relate the ISVD environment to the hypothesized ISED environment, we sought to insure that our ISED was designed to cause the ISVD functions to relate to assimilation (by the student-user) of the known. We tried, in this way, to design the hypothesized in terms of the known, and to indicate the extensions upon the known that we regarded as necessary for the existence of an operational ISED environment.

We think that not many people have dared to challenge educational research _per se_ in terms of its _capacity_ to _illuminate_ problems and understandings of _students_ so that they _grow_ in essentially self-correcting ways to become independent of judgmental functions and structures imposed by _others_. To achieve that objective would require that students, as well as professional educational researchers, become sophisticated in numeric analysis.

Although we are conscious of just how far we are from having a research-grounding educational machine, we think that we have cast a bright light on both education and educational research by our analysis of the design problem. That light came, we think, from a definition of educational research that involves the simultaneous education of the person being "educated" and the researcher conducting the investigation. Moreover, by acting _as if_ a research-grounding educational machine _could_ be constructed that would do this kind of educational research, we find that we have been forced to specify (as best

44

we can) what such a "machine" would have to be like. We regard that as no small achievement.

As we tried to specify what such a "machine" would be like, we capitalized on the obvious notion that an electronic computer is not one machine but many machines, and that it is in the writing of procedures for such a computer to follow that one, in effect, specifies and "creates" (via the computer) that "machine." The machine may not now exist. Perhaps, as far as our hypothesized research-grounding education machine is concerned, it need never exist. But to gain the tremendous advantage of this analysis one does need to think that such machines could exist and would exist if they satisfied the functions outlined for them as a result of being programmed for those functions.

What we have tried to do has been to discipline ourselves to specify a procedure that might clarify our understanding of what is involved in giving meaning to research in education. If we could accomplish that, we might narrow the gap that currently exists between research and education, as they are presently constituted. In attempting this, we consciously sought to expose our procedure, as well as our understanding. Understanding has been our object, and our means has been the description of procedures. Our product may well be a psychology, particularly an embryonic psychology, of the tacit mechanisms for acquisition of understanding, including (of course) an understanding of educational research itself.

As we have worked our way to this point, our most fundamental premise has been (and still is) not only that arrival at a particular decision about career choice is possible, but also that the general process of decision making can be accommodated within a human subject. We regard such an accommodation of the general decision-making process as a phenomenal feat, both literally and figuratively. It requires, as we see it, that one must be able to comprehend the principles of design in purpose well enough to deal with them somewhat as objects, even while being beset on all sides during the decision-making process by their individually subjective effects. Realization and acceptance of this "power" (or ability) opens one up for an interactive life. Dealing with reasoning and thought as if there were a "machine" in a person brings this functional potential of man qua man (person qua person) closer to the perceptual surface than we think has been possible before.

* * * * * * * * * * * * * * * *

S E C T I O N II

PERSONALITY AS A CONSTRUCTION

OF

THE MATHEMATICAL GROUP:

THE EDUCATION MACHINE AT WORK

AN OVERVIEV

* * * * * * * * * * * * * * * *

SECTION II

PERSONALITY AS A CONSTRUCTION OF THE MATHEMATICAL GROUP:
THE EDUCATION MACHINE AT WORK

AN OVERVIEW

In this second section we seek credibility for what we
call a group constructionist theory of personality construction.
We do that by taking two steps forward. The first and main
step is to introduce the group theory of personality, which we
do by presenting the concept of the personality group advanced
by Ernest M. Ligon in 1968. Then we proceed to revise Ligon's
group structure to achieve a more logically esthetic organization of its elements. However, as we refine Ligon's basic

thesis, we maintain a theoretical organization which is isomorphic with his original structure.

The second step is to introduce additional theory, which we unite with Ligon's into a basically empirical structure. For instance, we call upon the theory of mathematical groups to suggest properties which exist in theory, but need to be tested in the natural order of things. In our view, alternating appeal to the general (to suggest a test of the specifics) with study of inconsistencies between specifics and the generalities (to tell us what requires further investigation) constitutes the essence of being scientific about what one holds to be true in the natural order of things. The six chapters in Section II illustrate our use of that process.

In these six chapters we illustrate, also, what the design of an operating Education Machine would cause us to do as we interacted with it in the realm of personality, given the data and the experience of the Union College Character Research Project and the structure of Ligon's group. For example, we can imagine our process of discovery as an interchange between such an Education Machine (which we designed in Section I) and an Inquirer (such as we are). To illustrate this idea, imagine the following extended interaction between the Education Machine and an Inquirer who set out, as we did, to discover structure and order in human personality.

Inquirer:	(Inquirer connects terminal to the Education Machine and proceeds to identify himself or herself to the Machine.)
	Hello. This is _____.
	Are we connected?
Education Machine:	Welcome, _____.
	You are now connected with the Education Machine.
	What would you like to do?
Inauirer:	I would like to consider human personality.
	Can you help me to do that?
Education Machine:	Fine. Do you want to know what I have already stored in my memory, or do you have something else you want to do?
Inquirer:	I will want to draw on your memory, but I do have something else that I really want to do.
	Is that all right?
Education Machine:	Certainly.
	What about human personality would you like to consider?
Inquirer:	I want to consider whether there is order in the evident complexity of human personality.
	Can you help me?
Education Machine:	I think so.
	Are you interested in order as lawfulness alone, or are you interested in order as an indication of presumed structure in human personality?
Inquirer:	I am interested in order as an indication of presumed structure.
	Please proceed.

Education Machine:	All right. I can help you do that.
	Do you want to specify either a structure or a structural analog, or do you want to learn what I have stored in memory?
Inquirer:	I think I want to start with what you can tell me, in very general terms, about the presumed structure of human personality.
	Will you do that for me?
Education Machine:	Certainly. In very general terms, human personality is a construct that exhibits both complexity and continuity. Therefore, human personality is all too likely to be confusing to human beings.
	(The printout continues with the substance of the text as provided in Chapter 2, pages 71 through 72.)
	Do you want, at this point, to specify either a structure or a structural analog?
Inquirer:	Yes.
	What would happen if I posited that the structure of human personality was like the result of a factor analysis?
Education Machine:	Thank you.
	You have supplied a structural analog.
	Therefore you wish to reason analogically. Factor analysis will be accepted as an analog for the structure that may be posited for human personality.
	(The printout continues with the substance of the text as provided in Chapter 2, pages 72 through 76.)
	What would you like to do now?
Inquirer:	I am not sure.
	What can I do?

Education Machine:	You can use my considerable computational facility, which is programmed within a logic that is designed to help you move interactively from the specific to the general.
	You will, of course, have to evolve those generalities, but I can help you by prompting you to seek them and to get them.
	What would you like to do now?
Inquirer:	That sounds good.
	However, in order to evolve such generalities, what do I have to do next?
Education	How about giving me some data to work on for you?
	Do you have any such data to load at this time?
Inquirer:	I think so.
	However, can you suggest any criteria for my data?
Education Machine:	Yes, I can suggest criteria for your data.
	The data you want to load should be about humans, and it should be concerned with what humans believe to be personality.
	If you also have a hunch that the data might fit in your structural analog, that would help.
Inquirer:	Thanks.
	I have noted your suggestions about criteria.
	What kinds of data can you accept and work upon for me?
Education Machine:	I can accept either numeric or alphabetic data.
	However, you must specify a format.
	I can also accept combinations of numeric and alphabetic data, depending (again) on the format in which you tell me to expect the data when you load it.
	Do you need more information?

Inquirer:	I do not think so.
	I have a combination of numeric and alphabetic data that is set in the context of journal articles, research reports and research notes.
	Can you accept such data, even if much of it is prose?
Education Machine:	I think so, if I understand you correctly.
	Please proceed to load your data.
Inquirer:	Thank you.
	I am proceeding to load data from the Union College Character Research Project of Schenectady, New York. (N.B.*)
	My data are now loaded.
	Have you accepted them?
Education Machine:	I have examined and accepted your data. They are a combination of alphabetic and numeric data, much of which is in the form of prose, which is found in articles in the journal Character Potential: A Record of Research, plus a number of research reports and some research notes from the Union College Character Research Project staff and its director, Ernest M. Ligon.
	I now have your data in a number of separate files. If you wish, you may access the files separately, or you may access all of the data under the heading of the LIGON DATA set. If you wish me to work upon the whole body of data, please refer to it as the LIGON DATA set in making your request.

---

*(N.B.: (Note: For clarification of "N.B." see page 114 of Chapter 4.) This is obviously a big step. It presumes that the Inquirer or, in this instance, the authors not only have data but can, as well, adopt a format that will prove useful for the interaction that is desired. In reality, the authors know the movement from data to format usually is a matter that occurs iteratively.)

Education Machine:	If you wish to refer to specific files within the LIGON DATA set, please ask for a listing of the files and, then, refer to a file by name.
	What do you want to do next?
Inquirer:	I would like to observe the historical development of the data in the LIGON DATA set.
	Can you help me do that?
Education Machine:	Yes.
	I can sequence data by date, and I can observe trends. However, within what parameters do you want me to operate? For example: Developmental Psychology, Mathematics, General Psychology, History of Science. Please specify one or more parameters.
Inquirer:	Sorry.
	Use as your basic parameters: Piagetian Theory, Mathematics (especially Group Theory), Logic and Theoretical Psychology.
	Can you now review the historical development of the LIGON DATA set for me?
Education Machine:	Thank you for giving the parameters for me to use.
	I can now proceed.
	Consider, if you will, that the idea of structure is no stranger to theoretical psychology.
	(The printout continues with the substance of the text as provided in Chapter 3, pages 77 through 84.)
	Can I do anything more for you?
Inquirer:	Yes, I think so.
	Can you give me a list of references within the LIGON DATA set that you used, plus any other resources you used to observe this historical development?

| Education | Certainly. |
| Machine: | |

(The printout produces the references noted in the text of Chapter 3, plus copies of two figures.)

Do you wish to continue your search for structure in human personality using the LIGON DATA set as a base?

Inquirer: Yes.

I also want to check my perception of the materials you have just shown me from the LIGON DATA set.

Can you help me?

| Education | I think so. |
| Machine: | |

What is your perception that you want me to check?

Inquirer: I perceive that the inter-element interactions in the two figures in the LIGON DATA set are similar, but one of the figures is more highly ordered or structured than the other.

Am I correct?

| Education | You are correct in your perception. |
| Machine: | |

What would you like to do now?

Inquirer: I am curious.

I want to discover what is really going on in the Ligon Group Model. Also, I would like to be able to specify that (as I do this) I am generating information for an even more inclusive category, which I would like to call the GROUP MODEL set of data. Therefore, I want to include the LIGON data set within the GROUP MODEL set of data, without confusing my discoveries with the data from the LIGON DATA set.

Can I do that?

Education Machine:	I think you can do what you want to do.
	However, let me check to be sure that I understand what it is that you do want to do. As I understand it:
	You wish to discover a maximum order to the set of interactions posited by the figures in the LIGON DATA set, without losing the possibility of interrelating what you discover with the basic data you supplied to me. You want to call a larger, inclusive category the GROUP MODEL set of data.
	Do I correctly understand what you want to do?
Inquirer:	Yes. You have understood me correctly.
	What else can you help me to do?
Education Machine:	Since you have supplied the parameters of Mathematics and Logic, I could help you discover whether there is some general order or pattern to the interactions in the two figures you have identified.
	Would you be interested in doing that?
Inquirer:	Yes.
	Please help me to discover the maximum order or pattern, in terms of both the specifics of the LIGON DATA set and of some general order or pattern that may be posited of the set of inter-element interactions displayed by both figures in the LIGON DATA set.
	Please proceed.
Education Machine:	All right.
	Your instructions are accepted. Consider that:
	If one imagines that order is related to concepts such as pattern and regularity, then the discerning of order in any complexity means finding a way to highlight whatever inherent pattern or regularity may in fact exist in the complexity.
	(The printout continues with the substance of the text of Chapter 4, pages 92 through 100.)

Education Machine:	If one accepts the apparently reasonable proposition that what is reported in the LIGON DATA set as Tables 3.1 and 3.2 is also represented in the GROUP MODEL set as Tables 4.1 and 4.2, then one may ask what kind of group it is that is represented by the various interaction tables.
	Are you interested in doing that?
Inquirer:	Yes, I am interested in doing that.
	Please proceed.
Education Machine:	This question includes, of course, the question whether, in fact, these groups are mathematical groups at all.
	(The printout continues with the substance of the text of Chapter 4, pages 100 through 105.)
	The goal of a general description of the group structure model of personality has, it seems, been reached. It is possible to understand quite readily and mathematically the nature of the interactions posited by the figures in the LIGON DATA set. With this accomplishment it is now possible to move on to look at the specifics of the Group affirmed by Tables 3.1 in the LIGON DATA set and ask and decide some basic questions about the group structure model of personality.
	Do you wish to continue?
Inquirer:	Yes. I do wish to look at the specifics in the original data supplied to you in the LIGON DATA set, and I do wish to ask specific and basic questions of these data.
	Please proceed.
Education Machine:	Thank you.
	Please consider the following observations:
	Since the tables displayed in Tables 4.1, 4.2 and 4.4 are isomorphic, it seems reasonable to look at the principles used to construct the abstract group affirmed by Table 4.1 that is isomorphic to the abstract group of Table 4.4.

Education Machine:	Do you follow what I am proposing?
	Do you want me to go on?
Inquirer:	I am not certain that I follow what you are doing. However, I do want you to go on doing it anyway.
	Please proceed.
Education Machine:	All right. I will continue along the line I have initiated.
	We should be able to set up a series of symbol substitution conventions that would equate the specific elements of Table 4.1 with specific elements symbolized in Table 4.4.
	(The printout continues with the substance of the text of Chapter 4, pages 105 through 113.)
	The symbol substitution conventions of Figure 4.6 suggest that there is a need for definitional statements for each of the sixteen elements of the group structure model.
	Do you agree to this need?
Inquirer:	Yes.
	I do agree that the elements need definitional statements.
	Can you proceed?
Education Machine:	Yes.
	I can proceed a little further.
	Shall I do so?
Inquirer:	Please proceed.
Education Machine:	This need for element definitions has probably been evident for some time, and the attempt to discover and use a criterion for marginal sequencing merely made the need more obviously evident.
	(The printout continues with the substance of the text of Chapter 4, page 113.)

Education Machine	Considering what you now know about the set of elements in the group structure model of personality, are you prepared to create definitional statements for the several elements?
Inquirer:	I think so. However, let me check something out with you. Can I leave the element titles unchanged from what they were in the LIGON DATA set and still submit definitional statements for the several elements, based on my understanding of the phenomena referred to by each element?
Education Machine:	I can accept such pairs of element titles and definitional statements by filing them in the GROUP MODEL set. This would leave unchanged the original statements in the LIGON DATA set. Will that be satisfactory to you?
Inquirer:	Yes. That would be quite satisfactory. I am loading a set of definitional statements at this time. (At this point, the Inquirer might load a set of definitional statements that would be substantially those found at the end of Chapter 4, pages 113 through 119.) Have you accepted the definitional statements I have loaded?
Education Machine:	I have accepted sixteen pairs of definitional statements and element titles, which titles are identical to those found in the original data supplied to me. These pairs are now part of the GROUP MODEL set in my memory. Do you want to do anything else?
Inquirer:	Yes. I think I do want to do some more. However, would you review for me what I have done so far, with your help?

Education Machine:	Surely.
	The somewhat gutsy question – What the hell is going on here? – can be interpreted as a pointed expression of the general evaluative question.
	(The printout continues with Chapter 5, page 121.)
	Now what would you like to do?
Inquirer:	Can you help me look for implications of what I have done so far?
Education Machine:	I can, if you help me by specifying more exactly what it is that you want me to do.
	What are your instructions?
Inquirer:	Compare and contrast the LIGON DATA set interaction tables with the various interaction tables generated as a part of the GROUP MODEL set. Use the parameters that I have already supplied.
	Please proceed.
Education Machine:	Thank you.
	Your instructions are accepted. Consider the following:
	The criterion-sequenced Set of sixteen elements is displayed in an interaction table in Table 5.1.
	(The printout continues with the substance of the text of Chapter 5, pages 121 through 123.)
	Shall I continue?
Inquirer:	Yes, do continue.
Education Machine:	I am sorry.
	What do you want me to do?
Inquirer:	Please proceed.
Education Machine:	Thank you.
	I am proceeding. Consider the following:

Education Machine:	If one assumes, as it seems reasonable to do, that the seven generalizations mentioned above are applicable to the criterion-sequenced group, then, through a process of successive pairings, one can readily discern a series of levels of group-ness implicit in this particular Abelian group of order sixteen.
	(The printout continues with the substance of the text of Chapter 5, pages 123 through 127.)
	The group-ness of each level means that the group properties are pervasive in the model. That makes the model powerful. That also makes the problem of construct identification and titling important, as well as possible.
	Do you agree or disagree?
	Shall I continue, or shall I stop?
Inquirer:	If I follow what you have done so far, I agree.
	I also want you to continue.
	Please proceed.
Education Machine:	Thank you.
	I am proceeding. Consider this observation:
	With my help you have now identified a maximum order and pattern, including a group-inherent hierarchical structure of levels of constructs. This information is all now stored in my most general and inclusive category, the GROUP MODEL set of data.
	What do you want to do now?
Inquirer:	Are the various group-inherent constructs in the hierarchical structure of levels of constructs titled?
Education Machine:	No. As yet, they are not titled.
	Up to this point, they are only identified as logical implications of the sixteen element group developed as a part of the GROUP MODEL set.
	Would you care to give titles to those constructs?

Inquirer:	All right, I'll supply titles.
	How do I do that?
Education Machine:	Consider Figure 5.1 in your copy of the printout.
	As I ask you for a title of a construct, please type in your choice. I will specify a construct by the abstract symbol found in parentheses underneath the underlined descriptive phrase.
	Are you ready to proceed?
Inquirer:	Yes, I am ready.
	Please proceed.
Education Machine:	Thank you.
	I will start at the top of Figure 5.1. What is your title for the construct symbolized as (1"")?
Inquirer:	Since that construct is the most holistic, I want to give it the title of PERSONALITY.
Education Machine:	Good.
	The construct symbolized as (1"") is now entitled PERSONALITY.
	Let me move down one level. What do you wish to title the construct symbolized as (1'")?
Inquirer:	Let me see. The construct (1'") functions as an identity element in a mathematical group with one generator element. I know! I want to give construct (1'") the title PERSON.
Education Machine:	Good.
	The construct symbolized as (1'") is now entitled PERSON.
	Next, what do you want to title the construct (a'")?
Inquirer:	As I see it, my problem is to title the subconstruct that functions with PERSON to constitute the holistic construct I have entitled PERSONALITY.
	Is my logic in order?

63

Education Machine:	Your logic is in order.

What do you wish to call the construct symbolized as (a'")?

(N.B.: This process of construct titling would, of course, continue until all of the thirty-one constructs in the hierarchical structure of Figure 5.1 were titled. Since titling is an inherently arbitrary procedure, the Education Machine cannot supply titles on its own. The Machine defines the constructs solely in terms of the abstract symbols and relationships. Titles are matters of human convenience.)

All of the constructs in Figure 5.1 have now been titled.

Would you like to see the result of your work?

Inquirer: Yes.

Please display the results of my titling for me.

Please proceed.

Education Machine: Thank you.

Here are the results of your titling of the thirty-one constructs found in Figure 5.1.

(The printout continues and displays Figure 6.1, as found in Chapter 6, page 130.)

What do you want to do now?

Inquirer: I would like to explore the evident implications of what I have just done by titling the various constructs in this hierarchical structure model of human personality.

Can you help me do that?

Education Machine: Certainly.

However, you must supply me with some instructions.

Do you want me to start with any particular one of the numbered Levels of Figure 6.1?

Inquirer:	All right. Here are my instructions:
	Please start with Level I and work downwards to Level IV. Identify the interrelationships posited by the GROUP MODEL set, as it now stands.
	Please proceed.
Education Machine:	Thank you.
	The hierarchy of constructs displayed in Figure 6.1 locates the most general and most inclusive construct in Level I, and terms it PERSONALITY.
	(The printout continues with the substance of the text of Chapter 6, pages 129 through 135.)
	Before I proceed further, I have a question for you:
	Can I generate a series of alphabetic abstract symbols for the thirty-one construct titles you have supplied to me?
Inquirer:	I suppose so.
	Will it really help?
Education Machine:	Such symbol conventions will enable me to specify the inter-construct relationship in a more formal manner. This will introduce a degree of symbolic elegance, but it is primarily a convenience.
	Do you agree or disagree?
Inquirer:	I agree.
	Please proceed.
Education Machine:	Thank you.
	I shall generate alphabetical abstract symbols for the thirty-one constructs you titled for Figure 6.1.
	(The printout continues with the substance of the text of Chapter 6, pages 135 through 138.)
	Are you interested in the possibility of mixed, inter-Level combinations?

Inquirer: I really do not know.

                   However, since I am interested in almost anything
                   about this process, do tell me what you have dis-
                   covered about such mixed combinations.

                   Please proceed.

Education   Thank you.
Machine:
                   The symbol + was proposed for the inter-Level re-
                   lationship of "constituting" in the group struc-
                   ture model.

                   (The printout continues with the substance of the
                   text of Chapter 6, page 138.)

                   Do you want me to do something else for you?

Inquirer: Yes. I think so.

                   Can you help me discover a process that is very
                   general that will account for the process of "con-
                   stituting" as one moves up from the more specific
                   Levels to the more general Levels of the group
                   structure model?

Education   I think that I can help you.
Machine:
                   If my data analysis and logic analysis functions
                   have been correctly programmed, it should be pos-
                   sible to do what you seem to be asking. There-
                   fore, see if the following makes sense to you:

                   In Figure 4.4 an abstract group of order sixteen
                   isomorphic with the maximum inherent order of the
                   original group of elements was displayed.

                   (The printout continues with the substance of the
                   text of Chapter 6, pages 138 through 141.)

                   Would you like to review what you have done
                   recently?

Inquirer: Yes. I think so.

                   Could you give me a composite picture of the hi-
                   erarchical structure of constructs, as it now
                   exists in the GROUP MODEL set?

66

Education Machine:	Certainly. (The printout continues with the substance of the text of Chapter 6, pages 141 through 143, plus Figure 6.4.) Would you care to have me comment further on what has just been displayed for you?
Inquirer:	Yes. Please proceed.
Education Machine:	Thank you. Consider that: One can readily see that the common term associated with each of the constructs in Levels I, II, III and IV tends to become more complex, albeit it does so in an ordered manner, as one conceptually moves up from Level IV toward Level I. (The printout continues with the substance of the text of Chapter 6, pages 141 through 147.) Is there anything more you would like to do with the GROUP MODEL set at this time?
Inquirer:	Yes. I think there is. I would like to see if the phenomenon of human friendship can be modeled by the group structure I have been exploring so far. Can you do that for me?
Education Machine:	I have created a separate file entitled FRIEND-SHIP, but you must supply some data before I can compare and contrast that file with the GROUP MODEL set. Do you have such data?
Inquirer:	Is your file FRIENDSHIP really without any data?
Education Machine:	You are correct. My file FRIENDSHIP is now empty, until you supply me some data on the phenomenon that you want to use under this title. Please load your data now.

Inquirer:	All right.
	I am now loading data on the phenomenon of human friendship. The data are in the form of a series of questions and answers. The subject of the data is the degrees of human friendship.
	(At this point, the Inquirer loads the dialogue found in Chapter 7, pages 149 through 150.)
	Can you handle that data?
Education Machine:	Thank you.
	I have received your data and filed them in my file entitled FRIENDSHIP. The data you have supplied are in the form of several prose passages that constitute a series of questions and answers. I can handle your format.
	If you wish, I can now examine your data for the likelihood that the group structure model of personality can, in fact, model the human phenomenon described by your data.
	Shall I proceed?
Inquirer:	Yes.
	Please proceed.
Education Machine:	Thank you.
	Friendship appears to be a persistent human phenomenon that admits of degrees, although it apparently is not a very precise construct.
	(The printout continues with the substance of the text of Chapter 7, pages 149 through 159.)
	My logic analysis has identified one very general comment that may be of interest to you.
	Shall I continue?
Inquirer:	Yes.
	Please proceed.

Education Machine:	Thank you.
	An implicit question raised by the group structure model presented previously is a very old question: What is Man?
	(The printout continues with the substance of the text of Chapter 7, pages 159 through 163.)
	The active and conscious participation of the human in such a process of re-construction of PERSONALITY seems to be a capability, a possibility, that involves a drastic extension of the operational range of human freedom and responsibility.
	Do you want to do anything more at this time?
Inquirer:	No. Not at this time.
	However, can you save the GROUP MODEL set of files and data, so that it will be available when I next sign onto the Education Machine?
Education Machine:	Yes. The GROUP MODEL set of files and data can be saved for you.
	Do you wish me to do that?
Inquirer:	Yes.
	Please save the GROUP MODEL set.
Education Machine:	The GROUP MODEL set of files and data are now SAVED. When you next sign onto the Education Machine you may access them under that title.
	Are you signing off from the Education Machine now?
Inquirer:	Yes. I am signing off at this time.
	Good bye.
Education Machine:	Good bye.
	It has been an interesting set of discoveries.
	I look forward to working with you again.
	CONCLUSION.

<u>SAVED</u>: GROUP MODEL set of data and files.

<u>MODE OF OPERATION</u>: Interactive

<u>LOGIC USED</u>: Formal and Analogical

<u>INQUIRER SUPPLIED PARAMETERS</u>:

Human personality

Order as an indicator of structure

Factor Analysis as a structural analog

Alphanumeric prose format for data

Trend analysis for historical development

Piagetian Theory

Mathematics (especially group theory)

Logic

Theoretical Psychology

GROUP MODEL as a supraordinate category

Maximum order and pattern

Definitional statements for 16 elements

Compare and Contrast

Identification of evident implications

Titles for 31 constructs in an hierarchy

Theoretical formality

Combinative possibilities

Periodic, composite review of progress

Modeling as a test of data-theory fit.

TERMINAL DOWN.

CHAPTER 2

THE POSSIBILITY OF STRUCTURE IN PERSONALITY

Personality exhibits both complexity and continuity and is therefore all too likely to be confusing. One need not be a great scholar, or an historian of the oft tangled web of psychological theory and practice, to recognize this generalization as a statement of some truth. We hope to dispel some of the confusion that surrounds the construct personality.

One may reasonably hypothesize that the confusion attendant upon the continuous complexity, or complex continuity, of personality may be responsible for many psychologists turning away from the construct. One can wonder whether the reductionist theories that have pushed this construct aside would have been so acceptable had personality been less complex. However, even if study and theory have sought to disregard the construct, (or to substitute other seemingly more satisfactory ones), the phenomenon has not disappeared. Personality continues to be a phenomenon that is complex and somewhat baffling, but marked by an evident continuity.

Evidence for continuity of personality comes from the common observation that people are aware of being themselves through time. This awareness, though commonplace, poses a hoary but still intriguing problem. Continuity is experienced and experienceable, but it is difficult to explain or understand.

Evidences for the complexity of personality, likewise, seem readily available. One has only to attempt to make behavioral descriptions of one's own actions to encounter the problem of complexity. When descriptions of another person's actions are attempted, the complexity and the problem become even more obvious. Although a person exists as a recognizable entity, it is rarely a simple one. Categorizing this problem as an expression of individual differences achieves little beyond an exchange of labels. The complexity is present, whether one observes one or one hundred persons. In fact, if one is sensitive to data for one hundred persons, one is likely to be even more aware of the complexity generated by the larger number of observations.

Humans experience the seemingly paradox of persistent, continued identification. They also demonstrate remarkable complexity as they encounter and tolerate a range of variation that often exceeds their most extravagant guesses. This multiple experience can lead one to imagine that underneath (or "behind," or "through") the complexity there is some general structure that accounts for the relative continuity and, yet permits a complexity of observed variation. So, while seeking to understand this elusive phenomenon, one is inclined to posit a structure for its existence.

In the preceding paragraphs, personality-as-encountered has been analyzed in broad brush strokes. The purpose was to suggest that personality-as-encountered requires one to posit the existence of some unknown but presumedly knowable structure. At this point, we wish to establish the point that structure is quite likely to be posited when one experiences or encounters human personality.

Once this point is accepted, the structure so posited becomes a major issue when one confronts the concept of personality. Despite the confusion often attendant upon study of personality, the nature of the posited structure is important. It influences one's further understanding of the phenomenon and the very language one uses to talk about personality. Thus, consideration of the structure which we presume to be expressed in personality-as-encountered offers an entree to an understanding of personality itself as a phenomenon.

FACTOR ANALYSIS

We propose that the analytical method of Factor Analysis offers an analog of such a structure. We also suspect that Factor Analysis is remarkably similar, at a rational and mathematical level, to what we tend to do intuitively when we attribute an unknown but knowable structure to the complex phenomenon of personality. In both instances a complex array of many "measures" or "impressions" is posited to be the result of interactions among more basic, powerfully affective factors. These factors provide a simpler conceptual structure, in terms of which the observed complexity can be understood. When successful, the positing of such a simpler conceptual structure offers a way to account for the complexity of a set of observations or impressions. Thus, one can then say that it is now easier to understand the phenomenon.

Without attempting to provide a summary of the historical development of the technique of Factor Analysis, we wish to consider the logical and empirical fundamentals of the method. We recall that initially it was consideration of the implications of the ability to construct large matrices of intercorrelated coefficients that led to the discovery of the technique of extracting common factors (Adcock, 1954).

As we understand it, calculation of a correlation coefficient is a way of stating mathematically the degree of mutual associativity that exists between pairs of measures. Thus, when a number of such measures are put into a matrix and the degree of mutual associativity between all possible pairs of measures is calculated, the result is the intercorrelation matrix. That matrix is, then, a mathematical picture of an associative network existing within the set of measures. Such a network consists of pairs with degrees of closeness of association that vary from a direct, positive covariation through neutrality to a direct, negative covariation.

An intercorrelation matrix presents a network of inter-measure associativity in which the overall pattern of coefficients reveals clusterings within a set of measures. Within a small matrix one often can recognize a pattern through simple direct observation, especially if one takes sufficient time to study the matrix itself. However, it is also possible to determine mathematically which sets of paired measures tend to be most closely associated with one another. Much of the history of Factor Analysis relates to a search for a mathematical technique to accomplish this end. The need for such a mathematical solution follows logically upon creation of a network of associations within a complex matrix.

The techniques of Factor Analysis make it possible to identify subsets of associated pairs of measures within a larger network. Since the number of such subsets will be smaller than the number of original measures entered into the intercorrelation matrix, the result of a Factor Analysis is a simplification of the original complexity. Conceptually, each member of a subset of measures identified by this process relates to something which the members have in common. This common something is termed a Factor.

The Factor posited as a common something shared by all measures in a subset is assumed to be influencing, operating through or controlling the measures in some way, as well as affecting the things that presumably have been measured. This assumption, in turn, enables one to understand the subset of measures as a whole (i.e., as an expression of the identified Factor). If the number of Factors that are so identified is drastically smaller than the original number of measures, then the original matrix is obviously simplified and, to that extent, becomes more readily understandable. However, if the original complex is genuinely large (i.e., if the number of original measures is actually quite extensive), then relatively little simplification results from use of this form of Factor Analysis. That is, a large number of subsets may remain, so the simplification is only evident when results are compared with the original complex of measures. However, one is not left without further recourse.

The technique of Factor Analysis is conceptually based upon a network of associativity. This concept is not discarded when a set of subsets is identified since the result may be conceptualized as a "new" set of subsets, a relatively simpler network of associativity, but still controlling or influencing in its effect. Thus, if the technique of Factor Analysis is applied iteratively, it would, theoretically, result in achievement of complete simplicity.

What has been described is termed a first order Factor Analysis. What has been suggested is a second order Factor Analysis which would, via iteration, treat the set of subsets of original measures in the same way the first order Factor Analysis treated the set of original measures. Such a second order Factor Analysis would begin with the network of associativity created by the first order Factors. That is, the creation of an intercorrelation matrix of Factors, rather than original measures, would allow the technique to be used once more. The result of this procedure would be to identify subsets of Factors that exhibit a relationship to some common something by virtue of their degree of association with one another. That common something could, then, be posited to be a second order Factor that, presumedly, was responsible for the degree of association between the subset of first order Factors constituting the second order Factor. In this way, a still smaller set of subsets of first order Factors could be identified and, therefore, the possibility of offering an even simpler way of understanding the original complex of measures might be achieved.

The important technical decisions to be made along the way--e.g., the values to be assigned as communalities in the intercorrelation matrix--have not been raised. These decisions are important, of course, and we would not wish to deny that fact (Guertin & Bailey, 1970). However, our present purpose is solely to present a conceptualization of Factor Analysis in sufficient detail to enable a reader to understand our desire

to use that methodology as an analog for the posited structure
of human personality.

TRAITS

We would suggest that the fundamental purpose of Factor
Analysis is to determine a structure of "traits" to which the
"traits" are subordinate to others in a hierarchical organization of associations. Such a structure is a matter of induction
or inference from an examination of the network of associations
among the "traits," of course. Once such a structure of
"traits" has been identified, it is logically construed to
represent that through which the "traits" themselves were
formed. The presumption is that the traits per se are derived
from the identified structure of Factors. It is this presumption which makes the technique of Factor Analysis so useful
when one tries to understand a complex entity such as human
personality.

However, the fact that the technique continually works
with what we have termed a network of associativity must not be
forgotten. The reason this fact must be kept in mind is simply
that, in reality, regardless of how "trait" and Factor are
logically related as supraordinate and subordinate constructs,
it is the combination of "trait" and Factor, taken together as
mutually interactive, that leads toward an understanding of the
structure and, thereby, of the original complex of measures
picturing some phenomenon. Thus, if we posit that personality
is modeled by a factorial structure, this last statement is an
important and necessary consideration if we are to understand
the complex phenomenon we call personality.

COMPLEXITY OF INTERRELATIONSHIPS

We are aware that in Factor Analysis the first order factors are ordinarily defined as linear functions of the "traits"
from which they were empirically derived. The same assumption
of linearity is often made of second order Factors. This assumption means that all variables (or measures, or "traits")
are presumed to relate additively to one another. Ordinarily,
only the mathematical relationship of addition or its mirror
image, subtraction, are invoked in either first order or second
order Factor Analysis. We suspect that this ordinary assumption
must be replaced, if our understanding of the complex phenomenon
we term personality is to be advanced materially. Therefore,
we propose to conceptualize inter-"trait," inter-element, and
inter-measure relationships as being more complex than those
modeled by linear functions.

An example of such a conceptualization appears in the relationships that Ernest M. Ligon of the Union College Character Research Project found among a set of personality traits he was using (Ligon, 1969, 1970). Ligon believed that those traits, as a set, functioned as if they were a mathematical group. We pause, therefore, to examine Ligon's model and to introduce the reader to it, for we need that model, as well as our analog of first order and second order Factor Analysis, to move on to our own proposal for a group theory of personality organization and, then, on to our proposal for a group theory of self-constructionist personality organization.

We believe that, although the pathway may be long, the result achieved may be a simplification sufficient to advance understanding of a phenomenon as complex as personality in the human being. We find that possibility genuinely fascinating. Therefore, we invite the reader to share our search, to think about what we propose and, then, to extend the results beyond our present limitations.

CHAPTER 3

ERNEST M. LIGON'S INSIGHT INTO
A GROUP THEORY MODEL OF PERSONALITY

The idea of structure is no stranger to theoretical psychology. However, utilization of the structure of a mathematical group does appear to be somewhat of a stranger. It was just over fifty years ago that Cassius J. Keyser, an American mathematician, proposed to psychologists the possibility of group structure in psychology by stating:

> I wish to propose for your future consideration a psychological question—one which psychologists (I believe) have not considered and which, though it has haunted me a good deal from time to time in recent years, I am not prepared to answer confidently. The question is: Is mind a group? (Keyser, 1922/1956)

Keyser may have asked the question of the wrong audience—mathematicians instead of psychologists—or when he asked it there may have seemed to be no reasonable answer. Although the question of a group structure was thus introduced, it has floated about the edges of theoretical psychology and little has been done to answer it.

While Jean Piaget's recurring use of the mathematical group in his theorizing about genetic epistemology is not to be taken as an answer to Keyser's question, his work made use of the structure of the group. As Piaget developed his own theory of the development of intellectual operations, he made use of the structure of the group in conjunction with what he called the calculus of logic. This usage found its most succinct and mathematical expression in Piaget's lectures in 1952 at the University of Manchester (Piaget, 1953). In those three lectures Piaget explored the usefulness of a set of logical transformations that had the properties of a group, and proposed that these transformations were useful for the psychological theorist. However, Piaget's concern seems to have been to use group theory to understand the propositional logic that, implicitly or explicitly, he regarded as a marker of formal operations. Thus, the structure of a group was used, but not quite in the way Keyser's question suggested.

Introduction of the theory of the group into psychological discourse, however, was a step toward the overarching, theoretical question raised by Keyser. Thus, the situation vis-a-vis the theory of groups is only slightly more advanced now than it was when Keyser first asked his speculative question. Perhaps in the 1970's psychologists will be able not only to ask the question again but also to be venturesome enough to propose an answer. If this were to occur, theoretical psychology would have a "new" and powerful conceptual tool to aid its acknowledged desire for structure.

ELEVEN GENERAL SUPER CLUSTERS

Although not a well-known structuralist, Ernest M. Ligon, the Director of the Union College Character Research Project, seems to have drawn inspiration from Piaget's work, since both men tried to use the theory of groups to organize seemingly complex phenomena. For instance, in 1967-1968 Ligon reviewed his work of over thirty years. During the process he came to suspect that group theory could accomplish for him what E. T. Bell had claimed for groups in 1951: "Wherever groups disclose themselves, or could be introduced, simplicity crystallized out of comparative chaos" (Bell, 1951/1956). Ligon's suspicion moved closer to certainty as the review continued. The review itself involved Ligon in identification of "an extensive list of research insights whose validity had been demonstrated by persistent usefulness over a long period of time" (Williams, 1970, p. 63). Having created a list of such "research insights," Ligon proceded to organize them through use of a method of cluster analysis into thirty-two clusters. Ligon then went on to recluster his thirty-two basic clusters into eleven more general super clusters.

SIXTEEN SUPER CLUSTERS

In attempting to interpret the nature of those eleven super clusters, Ligon, eventually, recognized that certain paired relationships among his super clusters seemed to suggest the behavior of the elements of a group. During the Summer of 1968 this insight led to the further recognition that four additional super clusters would be needed to make a coherent, powerful group structure. Therefore, he posited four additional or dummy super clusters, combined them with the eleven original super clusters, added "uniqueness", (which was posited to be the identity element in the group), and created an interaction table of sixteen super clusters. The four dummy super clusters turned out to be interpretable, when their theoretical interactions with the eleven original super clusters were considered as defining relationships (Williams, 1970).

In 1968 Ligon exposed his insight about the potential groupness of this set of sixteen super cluster "elements" (four interpreted dummy super clusters, eleven original super clusters, plus "uniqueness"). He spoke about the discerned group first to the Psychology Club of the State University of New York (Albany). Later that year he read a brief paper, "Exploring Character Development," at the 1968 meeting of the American Psychological Association in San Francisco, California. Still later that year he attempted to involve parents and adolescents in the use of what he had begun to assume was a general model to describe the development of human character, which he tended to define simply as "strength of personality" (Williams, 1970). He attempted this involvement through a series of four meetings in Honolulu, Los Angeles, Dallas, and Lansing.

For Ligon the group model of character or personality development was a beautifully simple way of expressing a complexity. He was apparently fascinated with group properties such as closure, an identity element (he believed that "uniqueness" functioned as such), the matter of an inverse (he considered each of the "elements" in the group to be its own inverse), and associativity. Ligon was attracted by the possibility that the group he was considering also had the property of commutativity. This led him to posit that the group of sixteen super cluster "elements" was an Abelian group: that is, that the group was, in fact, commutative (Ligon, 1970).

In the Summer of 1969 Ligon sought to involve adolescents in use of his group model of personality, which he now recognized had sixteen elements. He sought to do this through the device of a Youth Congress sponsored by the Union College Character Research Project and held on the campus of Union College in Schenectady, New York. One result of this attempt was a mimeographed document "Mathematical Group Theory. A Model for Personality Research" (Ligon, 1969). In that document Ligon published an interaction table for the sixteen element group that suggested four categories of four elements each. These categories were labeled as (a) Uniqueness Elements, (b) Short-term Elements, (c) Long-term Elements, and (d) Motivational Elements. Table 3.1 is a reproduction of Ligon's mid-1969 interaction table.

Table 3.1. Ligon's 1969 Interaction Table.

Inverses: (o) creative interaction   identity element   U

Row/column element labels (with inverses, subscript u): $S_u, E_u, V_u, R_u, D_u, W_u, M_u, C_u, J_u$ and $E_u, U, L_u, H_u, P_u, X_u, G_u, A_u$.

Column descriptors (vertical headings, in order):

Uniqueness Elements — Self-desires and Drives; Endowment; Resources; Vision of Destiny; Identity Element.
Short-term Elements — Uniqueness Roles Played; Toward Destiny; Learning Potentials and Skills; Decision-making; Skills; Home Lab.
Long-term Elements — Potentials; PS of One's; Broadening World; Philosophy of Values; Measurement of Character Pot.; Personality Methods of Evaluation.
Motivational Elements — Courage to Strive; Toward Max. Pot. Maturity of; Growth Potentials; Judgement and Wisdom; Action-investment of Energy Toward Destiny.

	Uniqueness Elements				Short-term Elements				Long-term Elements				Motivational Elements			
	S	E	V	U	R	L	D	H	W	P	M	X	C	G	J	A
U	S	E	V	[U]	R	L	D	H	W	P	M	X	C	G	J	A
S	[U]	V	E	S_u	L	R	H	D	P	W	X	M	A	J	G	C
E	V	[U]	S	E_u	H	D	L	R	M	X	W	P	J	A	C	G
V	E	S	[U]	V_u	D	H	R	L	X	M	P	W	G	C	A	J
[U]	S_u	E_u	V_u	[U]	R_u	L_u	D_u	H_u	W_u	P_u	M_u	X_u	C_u	G_u	J_u	A_u
R	L	H	D	R_u	[U]	S	V	E	C	A	J	G	W	X	M	P
L	R	D	H	L_u	S	[U]	E	V	A	C	G	J	P	M	X	W
D	H	L	R	D_u	V	E	[U]	S	G	J	A	C	X	W	P	M
H	D	R	L	H_u	E	V	S	[U]	J	G	C	A	M	P	W	X
W	P	M	X	W_u	C	A	G	J	[U]	S	E	V	R	D	H	L
P	W	X	M	P_u	A	C	J	G	S	[U]	V	E	L	H	D	R
M	X	W	P	M_u	J	G	A	C	E	V	[U]	S	H	L	R	D
X	M	P	W	X_u	G	J	C	A	V	E	S	[U]	D	R	L	H
C	A	J	G	C_u	W	P	X	M	R	L	H	D	[U]	V	E	S
G	J	A	C	G_u	X	M	W	P	D	H	L	R	V	[U]	S	E
J	G	C	A	J_u	M	X	P	W	H	D	R	L	E	S	[U]	V
A	C	G	J	A_u	P	W	M	X	L	R	D	H	S	E	V	[U]

As in: Ligon, Ernest M. Mathematical Group Theory: A Model for Personality Research. Schenectady, New York: Union College Character Research Project, 1969, p. 10. (Mimeographed)

Ligon did pioneer work and, so he would use words and give them a meaning and, then, proceed to change the words or the meaning, as might be expected. He simply would not "settle" upon a single definition for any period of time, so chances are he might not even "own" the statements in 1976. However, to assist in interpretation and understanding of Ligon's thinking and the changes we introduce, Figure 3.1 contains in parallel columns Ligon's statements at two different times about the "nature" of the several elements in the parent group of Order 16.

Ligon was obviously very intrigued by what he persistently referrred to as "triads" of elements. In a 1970 article in the journal, Character Potential: A Record of Research, he stated that such "triads" were, ". . . sub-groups, each involving Uniqueness and three of the other fifteen elements" (Ligon, 1970, p. 73). Although it is implicit in this description of a "triad" that it is a sub-group consisting of four group elements, and so meets one of the properties of a parent group of Order 16, Ligon did not develop this idea. He was much more interested in what seemed to be a three-ness patterning of the interaction of the fifteen elements other than the identity element (uniqueness).

In 1970 Ligon published another version of an interaction table for a total group of sixteen elements. As an illustration of his article, "A Map for Character Development: Mathematical Group Theory," which appeared in the July, 1970 issue of Character Potential: A Record of Research, Ligon created an interaction table that he entitled, "The Integration Table by Elements and by Five Triads" (Ligon, 1970). His fascination with seeming triadic interaction of elements is evident in both the title of the table and in the arrangement of the elements along the margins of the table as presented in Table 3.2.

In this new table, Ligon arranged the elements so that the identity element was placed in the extreme right-hand column and on the extreme bottom row, while he arranged the remaining fifteen elements into five sets of three elements each. The sets of three elements represented five "triads" in which, apparently, Ligon had some a priori interest. Thus, while the basic interrelationships among the sixteen elements remained unchanged, the 1970 interaction table (Table 3.2) appeared to be quite different from the earlier 1969 interaction table (Table 3.1).

Ligon apparently was still not certain about the most appropriate order (if any) for an interaction table representing the group of sixteen elements (or super clusters of research insights). However, by 1970 he had become quite convinced of the generality of the group as a model of character or

Table 3.2. Ligon's 1970 Interaction Table.

		1 S	2 E	3 V	4 X	5 H	6 A	7 P	8 J	9 D	10 G	11 M	12 L	13 R	14 C	15 W	16 [U]
1	S	[U]	V	E	M	D	C	W	G	H	J	X	R	L	A	P	S
2	E	V	[U]	S	P	R	G	X	C	L	A	W	D	H	J	M	E
3	V	E	S	[U]	W	L	J	M	A	R	C	P	H	D	G	X	V
4	X	M	P	W	[U]	A	H	E	L	C	R	S	J	G	D	V	X
5	H	D	R	L	A	[U]	X	G	W	S	P	C	V	E	M	J	H
6	A	C	G	J	H	X	[U]	R	V	M	E	D	W	P	S	L	A
7	P	W	X	M	E	G	R	[U]	D	J	H	V	C	A	L	S	P
8	J	G	C	A	L	W	V	D	[U]	P	S	R	X	M	E	H	J
9	D	H	L	R	C	S	M	J	P	[U]	W	A	E	V	X	G	D
10	G	J	A	C	R	P	E	H	S	W	[U]	L	M	X	V	D	G
11	M	X	W	P	S•	C	D	V	R	A	L	[U]	G	J	H	E	M
12	L	R	D	H	J	V	W	C	X	E	M	G	[U]	S	P	A	L
13	R	L	H	D	G	E	P	A	M	V	X	J	S	[U]	W	C	R
14	C	A	J	G	D	M	S	L	E	X	V	H	P	W	[U]	R	C
15	W	P	M	X	V	J	L	S	H	G	D	E	A	C	R	[U]	W
16	[U]	S	E	V	X	H	A	P	J	D	G	M	L	R	C	W	[U]

82

personality. Part way through his presentation of the group as
a model, Ligon made the following assertion:

> If you are dealing with an essential personality dy-
> namic that does not seem to fit this Group Theory Model, do
> not conclude that this disproves the validity of the model.
> In all probability it can be incorporated into one of the
> elements of this group. There is strong reason to believe
> that all essential characteristics of personality are inher-
> ent in this model. (Ligon, 1970)

Ligon's confidence in the group as a model is obvious. He
seemed to believe that the model per se was inclusive and
utterly general. He apparently believed he had found that simplification of seeming chaos that Bell suggested would come
from recognition or introduction of the group concept. However, Ligon seemed more interested in exploring results of
sheer groupness than in refining definitions of the sixteen
elements in the group itself.

Perhaps, since the elements were actually super clusters—
clusters of clusters of research insights—suggestive titling
was all that could be done at the time. In his 1970 article
Ligon provided element titles, plus a considerable amount of
presumedly illustrative material vis-a-vis the several elements,
but very sparse definitions. This 1970 article actually continued Ligon's practice of arguing analogically, rather than
systematically. He offered an illustration and implied that the
reader would understand what a super element was because the
illustration showed how the element worked. While this way of
arguing may well lead to a feeling of rightness, a sense of
face validity, it is not quite a definition.

After Ligon had insightfully identified his group of sixteen elements, he was most interested in moving directly to
their use. At a point some years removed from Ligon's initial
insight, it is possible to appreciate his excitement without
discrediting him for not producing definitions. At best, the
1970 article contained a series of intriguing hints which
seemed worthy of further development, since they were based
upon over thirty years of persistent attention to the psychological problem of character or personality development.

PERSONALITY CONSISTS OF AN ABELIAN GROUP OF ELEMENTS

The basic insight that a set of elements seems to function
as a group—perhaps even an Abelian group—and, so, explains
the development of character or personality is actually quite
fascinating. We wish to accept this insight and work with it

as a clue to the way order may be established within the complexity of human personality. We hope to suggest further applications for the model and, along the way, to engage in its further systematization. Although we believe that the materials we propose to work with have properties Ligon did not realize, and we conceive of uses for the model he did not imagine or investigate, we do acknowledge our debt to him for the basic germinal idea that personality may consist of an Abelian group of elements of a relatively high order of generality.

Figure 3.1 contains Ligon's statements regarding the sixteen elements of his group, as presented in his 1969 paper and in his 1970 article. The 1969 paper "defined" or described each element in terms of end-points of a presumed integration continuum. The 1970 article "defined" or described each element in a somewhat more concise manner, although Ligon repeatedly uses the concepts of a "developmental process," "integration," "unique" and "uniqueness," and his own trademark phrase "potential." In the following chapters we record our own processes of discovery as we came to see an inherent order to the parent group of Order 16 and, thereby, to see definitional implications for the several elements. Our considered restatements of element definitions will be found at the conclusion of Chapter 4, "How to Get There From Here."

As Used in 1969	As Used in 1970
(S) Use of Self-image and basic drives	**Element SELF (S)**
Low integration end of variable: Immediate satisfaction of one's most urgent desires and drives is seen as an end in itself. Characteristic of integrated personality: Self accepting and able to use one's unqiue pattern of drives and desires to accomplish one's important long-range goals.	Self is a developmental process with which, using the strengths of (U)niqueness, one can produce a more effective use of his Self; his inner desires and drives.
(E) Use of Endowment Resources (physical, mental, emotional and social)	**Element ENDOWMENT RESOURCES (E)**
Low integration: Use of miscellaneous aptitudes and skills for impulsive, immediate purposes. Integrated: Well-developed and coordinated use of aptitudes and skills for fully integrated and long-range purposes.	This is a developmental process in the use of his aptitudes and skills, approaching his unique maximum potential integration of them.
(V) Vision of Destiny (short and/or long-term goals)	**Element VISION (V)**
Low integration: Instantaneous short-sighted reaction to each situation or circumstance without coordinated plan of execution (what I want to do today). Integrated: A continually modified plan of action, whereby daily activities are directed toward the highest goal or purpose one visualizes for himself in his world.	The stages (facets) of the increasing development of one's perception of what his life will achieve.

Figure 3.1. Ligon's 1969 and 1970 Definitional Statements. (Based on terminology and statements in Mathematical Group Theory: A Model for Personality Research, 1969, pp. 6-7 (Mimeographed) and "A Map of Character Development: Mathematical Group Theory" in Character Potential: A Record of Research, Vol. 5, Nos. 1 and 2, July, 1970, pp. 83, 86, 87, 89, and 91, by E. M. Ligon.)

85

As Used in 1969	As Used in 1970
(P) Philosophy of Values (as developed up to now)	Element PHILOSOPHY OF VALUES (P)
Low integration: Miscellaneous set of usually dogmatic rights and wrongs.	This is a process of developing value attitudes which increasingly influence one's approach to life.
Integrated: Definite fully developed philosophy of life, to which one is dedicated.	

- -

(W) Broadening World (as perceived and experienced by the individual)	Element BROADENING WORLD AS PERCEIVED (W)
Low integration: Impulsive, irrational perception of world around him, with little meaningful relationship among its parts.	This is a developmental process which determines, both how one broadens his world and what influence it has on his personality.
Integrated: A well-integrated picture of the world, as he knows it and how to deal with it.	

- -

(M) Measure of Character Potentials	Element MEASURES OF THE DIMENSIONS OF CHARACTER ORIENTATION (M)
Low integration: One's use of his character potentials (in inherent purposiveness, social aptitude, and dedication to values), toward miscellaneous, disconnected objectives.	This is a developmental process in recognizing the degree of one's purpose, value, and social orientation, and increasing its effectiveness.
Integrated: One's well-understood and well-planned use of his character potentials toward achieving maximum potential.	

- -

Figure 3.1 Continued

As Used in 1969	As Used in 1970
(X) Tools of Evaluation	**Element SKILLS AND HABITS OF EVALUATION (X)**
Low integration: Impulsive, self-centered, and inaccurate methods of evaluation.	A growing ability to evaluate the situations one meets in life with increasing accuracy and in terms of one's (U)nique personality.
Integrated: Mastery of scientific tools of evaluation and careful use of them, without regard to selfish aims.	

- -

(D) Decision-Making Tools	**Element DECISION-MAKING HABITS AND SKILLS (D)**
Low integration: Thoughtless decisions, usually on basis of personal opinions, desires and wishes.	A set of decision-making habits and skills, which can be developed through training in uniqueness and personality integration.
Integrated: Mastery of accurate decision-making skills, and objective, determined use of them.	

- -

(L) Learning Potentials and Character Integration	**Element LEARNING (L)**
Low integration: A set of miscellaneous, often inaccurate facts, frequently used on the spur of the moment to prove an already taken position.	Learning which is becoming a unique part of the individual's personality.
Integrated: An organized, planned program of learning, and mastery of relevant portions of it, before making decisions about it.	

- -

Figure 3.1 Continued

As Used in 1969	As Used in 1970
(R) Roles Played in Daily Life	**Element ROLES (R)**
Low integration: Accepting and playing many unrelated and often meaningless roles, with little or no regard to ultimate purpose.	A growing picture of the most important roles one can play in life and how best he can play them as a unique individual.
Integrated: The choice of roles leading to one's destiny, and making the roles which are thrust upon him lead to this end.	

- -

(H) Home Lab Potentials (home as a laboratory for life)	**Element HOME AS A LABORATORY FOR LIFE (H)**
Low integration: Haphazard reaction to "home" influence, whether in family or in other functional groups, with no outside purpose in mind.	This is a developmental process in which he gains skill in the use of his home as a laboratory of life, a skill which can now become more effective.
Integrated: A careful assessment of one's home potentials both in family and in other intimate functional groups, and planned use of them for training and pretesting.	

- -

(J) Judgment and Wisdom (toward achieving maximum potential)	**Element JUDGMENT AND WISDOM (J)**
Low integration: Judgment based only on one's opinion, and often adhered to dogmatically against all others.	This consists of the development of judgment from thoughtless impulses to depth of wisdom in personality.
Integrated: Judgment based on one's vision of his destiny and interpretation of the present toward achieving it.	

- -

Figure 3.1 Continued

Terms and Definitions

As Used in 1969	As Used in 1970
(C) Courage to Strive toward Maximum Potential Low integration: Tendency to do the popular or easiest thing, especially if this brings praise from others. Integrated: Determination to do the thing that constitutes one's best contribution toward what most needs to be done.	**Element COURAGE (C)** A growing determination to deal with life's situations with strength and skill regardless of the cost.
(A) Action (Use of one's flow of energy) Low integration: Disorganized actions resulting from momentary impulses. Integrated: Maximum potential, goal-directed use of energy.	**Element ACTION (A)** One's efficiency in the investment of his energy is a developmental process which, with the application of the group theory principle, can produce an increasingly effective program of purpose-directed action.
(G) Growth and Achievement of Maturity Low integration: Failure to utilize the achievement potential that the growth process provides. Integrated: Achieving the full potentials for one's developing growth patterns.	**Element GROWTH AND MATURITY (G)** A developing ability to use the Maturity Potentials that come from increasing growth.
(U) Uniqueness (Patterns of individual differences) Low integration: Miscellaneous, unintegrated individual differences. Integrated: Use of patterns of individual differences toward maximum potential.	**Element UNIQUENESS (U)** . . ., in our conception, uniqueness, to which we assign the symbol (U), is one's maximum personality potential. (p. 79)

Figure 3.1 Continued

CHAPTER 4

HOW TO GET THERE FROM HERE

Theories abound in the field of psychology. Some exalt personality and the individual, while others seem to submerge personality in a welter of variables and, as a result, almost lose the individual. When yet another theory or model is suggested, two prosaic questions are to be asked. First, one may ask, "Why should I pay attention?" Second, one may ask a somewhat more gutsy question, "What the hell is going on here?" Both questions are existentially real. We believe that we address both questions in the course of this work, but we separate our answers.

The first question is an invitation to share intent. While we feel no need to hide our intentions, we can at this point do little more than allude to them. Essentially, we believe that Sanford was correct when he wrote of the need to develop, ". . . a paradigm of research which respects the nature of man as a symbol-using, self-reflective creature who acts as well as behaves" (Sanford, 1970, p. x). We think that it is vital to ask the extent to which current models of what Sanford termed "researchable man" are either distortions of, or limitations upon, what is humanly possible.

We intend to present the group structure as a model of human personality that respects mankind's nature. We intend to present a less distorting and less limiting model of "researchable man." We intend to accomplish (or approach) these goals with the group structure model of personality. These are our intentions. They constitute our rationale for asking that the reader attend to what follows.

The second question is more gutsy, of course, for it can be interpreted as dealing specifically with the group structure model. We interpret it to be a pointed expression of the general evaluative question. Among other things, the question concerns the set of relationships affirmed by Tables 3.1 and

3.2. Specifically, one can ask what pattern of relationships is actually being affirmed by these Tables as a model of human personality.

This second question concerns evaluation and can be answered in two steps. First, one can identify the maximum inherent order within the specific group of Order 16 identified in the Tables. However, that is only the first step in the answer to the question of what _is_ going on. The second step involves identification of a thoroughly general procedure for creation of an abstract group that is isomorphic to the group of Order 16 displayed in both Tables 3.1 and 3.2. If this second step can be taken, and we believe it can, then the group structure model of personality has the possibility of being quite serviceable. This serviceability will come, in part, because of a freeing of the model from the circumstances of its birth. Such generality both frees the model _from_ a specificity and _for_ application to a range of specificities. We believe the model possesses these qualities of serviceability and generality.

We intend to deal with the second of our prosaic questions (What is going on here?) first. We propose to begin by explicating the group's maximum inherent order. Then we propose to identify a general procedure for creation of an abstract group isomorphic to that group. We intend to address ourselves to the first of our prosaic questions in subsequent chapters by identifying some implications of the group structure model of human personality.

FINDING ORDER IN THE GROUP STRUCTURE

If one imagines that order is related to concepts such as pattern and regularity, then the discerning of order in any complexity means finding a way to highlight whatever inherent pattern or regularity may in fact exist within it. The interaction tables of Tables 3.1 and 3.2 (Ligon, 1969 and 1970, respectively) hint at an order but do not highlight one. In fact, Table 3.2 represents something of a clouding of the order evident in Table 3.1, since, although specific interactions of elements in both Tables are identical, that fact is not immediately evident. Thus, one can better begin to search for pattern, regularity, and order in Table 3.1.

When one analyzes Table 3.1 with the search for pattern and regularity in mind, it is possible to discern a fairly high degree of order. For example, a number of _pairs_ of elements appear to interact so as to produce, in a regular pattern, another pair of elements. One can readily identify this phenomenon by looking at the interaction of the pair (Self-desires and

Drives) and (Endowment Resources) that is symbolized by the letters S and E and the pair (Philosophy of Values) and (Measurement of Character Potential) that is symbolized by the letters P and M, which produces the pair of elements (Perceived Situation of one's broadening World) and (Personality methods of Evaluation) that is symbolized by the letters W and X. The pair (Self-desires and Drives) and (Endowment Resources) that is symbolized by the letters S and E and the pair (Courage to strive toward maximum potential) and (Maturity of growth potentials) that is symbolized by the letters C and G also interact to produce the pair of elements (Action-investment of energy toward destiny) and (Judgment and Wisdom) that are symbolized by the letters A and J. It also is evident that the pair (Self-desires and Drives) and (Endowment Resources) that is symbolized by the letters S and E interact with the pair (Judgment and Wisdom) and (Action-investment of energy toward destiny) that is symbolized by the letters J and A so as to produce the pair (Courage to strive toward maximum potential) and (Maturity of growth potentials) that is symbolized by the letters C and G. In a similar way, the pair (Vision of Destiny) and the identity element (Uniqueness) that is symbolized by the letters V and U interact with the pair (Courage to strive toward maximum potential) and (Maturity of growth potentials) that is symbolized by the letters C and G and with the pair (Judgment and Wisdom) and (Action-investment of energy toward desiny) that is symbolized by the letters J and A in a pattern that is isomorphic to the pattern for the first set of pairings identified above from elements in Table 3.1.

These complicated observations suggest that the set of four elements identified in Table 3.1 as the "Uniqueness Elements" interacts in an ordered and regular pattern with the set of elements identified as the "Motivational Elements." This set-set interaction produces a matrix of elements, all of which belong to the set termed the "Motivational Elements." If this specific observation is generalized, it seems that there is an ordered, regular pattern of interactions, set versus set, which suggests that the set of "Uniqueness Elements" functions as an identity element for the set of "Motivational Elements." This generalization, in turn, suggests that there should be other inter-set interactions that would be isomorphic to the one just noted between these two sets of four elements each. This seems like a good clue to the order inherent in the group of Order 16 posited by the interactions displayed in Table 3.1. Another and equally fascinating clue is that the interactions show a regularity and pattern at both the level of pairs of elements and at the level of sets of four elements.

Further consideration of Table 3.1 suggests yet another clue to the ordered, regular pattern of interactions inherent in this group. This clue is found in the sequence of element products recorded under the first-position element in each set of four elements. If one were to imagine moving the element $\underline{U}$ to the position of column 1 and row 1 in the extreme upper left-hand corner of the matrix, then the sequence of elements for the two sets of four elements entitled the "Short-term Elements" and the "Long-term Elements" would appear to match the marginal order. Testing this clue involves taking several actions that might demonstrate the maximum order inherent in this group per se. That is, one can resequence the marginal order of the "Uniqueness Elements" set and then, let that order determine the internal marginal sequence for each of the other three sets of four elements through the interaction of the "Uniqueness Elements" set of elements with the first-position element in each of these other three sets of four elements each.

One further observation of order seems worth mentioning. In Table 3.1 the element occupying the first-position (i.e., the most extreme left-hand position within the set of four elements) in each of the three sets entitled "Short-term Elements," "Long-term Elements," and "Motivational Elements" (i.e., the three elements symbolized by the letters $\underline{R}$, $\underline{W}$ and $\underline{C}$) are so interrelated that any two elements interact to produce the third element. This clue can be checked by the reader.

These clues should make it possible to rearrange the marginal sequence of elements in the interaction table of Table 3.1 so that the resulting table of interactions would evidence an even more pronounced order. Just such a rearranging of the marginal sequences, using the clues identified above, is displayed in Table 4.1.

An examination of Table 4.1 indicates that the goal of pronounced order, pattern, and regularity was achieved. In fact, also indicated is that the clue regarding the inter-set interactions was true: a regularity of pattern is evident at the level of pairs of elements, at the level of sets of four elements, and at the level of sets of eight elements. Table 4.1 seems to display the maximum inherent order of the group. If that is so, that fact would strongly suggest that this is also the maximum inherent order for both Tables 3.1 and 3.2 as well.

The evident order in Table 4.1 can be generalized by substituting abstract mathematical symbols for the element-identifying symbols of capital letters. When such a symbol substitution is carried out, the result looks like Table 4.2, which, therefore, represents a general statement of the originally posited inter-element interactions in this group.

Table 4.1.   A Reordering of Ligon's 1969 Interaction Table.

U S E V	R L H D	W P M X	C A J G

U̲ S̲ E̲ V̲   R̲ L̲ H̲ D̲   W̲ P̲ M̲ X̲   C̲ A̲ J̲ G̲

	U S E V	R L H D	W P M X	C A J G	
U̲S̲E̲V̲	U S E V	R L H D	W P M X	C A J G	U̲S̲E̲
	S U V E	L R D H	P W X M	A C G J	
	E V U S	H D R L	M X W P	J G C A	
	V E S U	D H L R	X M P W	G J A C	
R̲L̲H̲D̲	R L H D	U S E V	C A J G	W P M X	R̲L̲H̲D̲
	L R D H	S U V E	A C G J	P W X M	
	H D R L	E V U S	J G C A	M X W P	
	D H L R	V E S U	G J A C	X M P W	
W̲P̲M̲X̲	W P M X	C A J G	U S E V	R L H D	W̲P̲M̲X̲
	P W X M	A C G J	S U V E	L R D H	
	M X W P	J G C A	E V U S	H D R L	
	X M P W	G J A C	V E S U	D H L R	
C̲A̲J̲G̲	C A J G	W P M X	R L H D	U S E V	C̲A̲J̲G̲
	A C G J	P W X M	L R D H	S U V E	
	J G C A	M X W P	H D R L	E V U S	
	G J A C	X M P W	D H L R	V E S U	

U̲ S̲ E̲ V̲   R̲ L̲ H̲ D̲   W̲ P̲ M̲ X̲   C̲ A̲ J̲ G̲

Uniqueness Elements	Short—term Elements	Long—term Elements	Motivational Elements

Table 4.2. A General Form of a Resequenced Interaction Table.

		1‴						a‴						(08)
		1″		a″			b″		c″					(04)
	1′	a′	b′	c′	d′	e′	f′	g′						(02)
	1	a	b	c	d	e	f	g	h	i	j	k	l	m	n	o	
1	1	a	b	c	d	e	f	g	h	i	j	k	l	m	n	o	1
a	a	1	c	b	e	d	g	f	i	h	k	j	m	l	o	n	a
b	b	c	1	a	f	g	d	e	j	k	h	i	n	o	l	m	b
c	c	b	a	1	g	f	e	d	k	j	i	h	o	n	m	l	c
d	d	e	f	g	1	a	b	c	l	m	n	o	h	i	j	k	d
e	e	d	g	f	a	1	c	b	m	l	o	n	i	h	k	j	e
f	f	g	d	e	b	c	1	a	n	o	l	m	j	k	h	i	f
g	g	f	e	d	c	b	a	1	o	n	m	l	k	j	i	h	g
h	h	i	j	k	l	m	n	o	1	a	b	c	d	e	f	g	h
i	i	h	k	j	m	l	o	n	a	1	c	b	e	d	g	f	i
j	j	k	h	i	n	o	l	m	b	c	1	a	f	g	d	e	j
k	k	j	i	h	o	n	m	l	c	b	a	1	g	f	e	d	k
l	l	m	n	o	h	i	j	k	d	e	f	g	1	a	b	c	l
m	m	l	o	n	i	h	k	j	e	d	g	f	a	1	c	b	m
n	n	o	l	m	j	k	h	i	f	g	d	e	b	c	1	a	n
o	o	n	m	l	k	j	i	h	g	f	e	d	c	b	a	1	o
	1	a	b	c	d	e	f	g	h	i	j	k	l	m	n	o	

	1′	a′	b′	c′	d′	e′	f′	g′	(02)
1″			a″			b″		c″	(04)
1‴					a‴				(08)
			1⁗						(16)

A consideration of Table 4.2 suggests the following seven generalizations about the group of Order 16 originally displayed in Tables 3.1 and 3.2. Taken together, these seven generalizations form a description of the inherent order, pattern, or regularity of the group. As such, they will be useful later in a consideration of this particular set of sixteen elements.

1. Elements may be placed in _pairs_ which then exhibit a high degree of order in their interactions with other similar pairs of elements.

2. Element pairs may be combined into _pairs of pairs_, or sets of four elements each, which then exhibit a high degree of order in their interactions with other similar pairs of pairs of elements.

3. Element pairs of pairs or sets of four elements may be combined into _two pairs of pairs of pairs_ of elements, or sets of eight elements, which then exhibit a high degree of order in their interactions with one another.

4. The high degree of order exhibited by the interactions of _eight pairs_ of elements is isomorphic with the pattern of inter-element interactions exhibited by the eight elements occupying the upper left-hand quadrant of the generalized interaction table in Table 4.2 (i.e., the elements symbolized as 1, a, b, c, d, e, f, and g).

5. The high degree of order exhibited by the interactions of _four pairs of pairs_ of elements is isomorphic with the pattern of inter-element interactions exhibited by the four elements occupying the upper left-hand quarter of the upper left-hand quadrant of the generalized interaction table in Table 4.2 (i.e., the elements 1, a, b, and c).

6. The high degree of order exhibited by the interactions of _two pairs of pairs of pairs_ of elements is isomorphic with the pattern of inter-element interactions exhibited by the two elements occupying the first and second row and column position in the upper left-hand corner of the generalized interaction table in Table 4.2 (i.e., the elements 1 and a).

7. The high degree of order exhibited by the interactions of a _total set of sixteen elements_ with itself is isomorphic with the pattern of interactions exhibited by the so-called neutral or identity element in the generalized interaction table in Table 4.2 (i.e., the element 1).

These seven generalizations about the group structure displayed in Table 4.2 are generalizations from a _specific_ group's _structure_ and, also, are generalizations about the _group_

Postulate or Theorem:	Statement of the Postulate or Theorem of Group Theory:	Example Taken From Table 4.1 Table:
First Postulate	Closure: X * Y defines a unique element in the set.	D * R = V X * R = G S * R = L
Second Postulate	Associativity: (X*Y)*Z = X*(Y*Z)	(S*R)*V = S*(R*V) (L)*V = S*(D) H = H
Third Postulate	Neutral/Identity Element: X * I = X, and I * X = X	H * U = H U * H = H
Fourth Postulate	The Inverse: For each X in the set there exists a unique element X', such that X'*X = I and X*X' = L.	D * D = U A * A = U S * S = U J * J = U
First Theorem	Every element in a sequence of powers is an element of the group.	E, E^2, E^3, E^4 E U E U
Second Theorem	The sequence of powers must be cyclical in nature.	R, R^2, R^3, R^4 R U R U
Third Theorem	Every cycle of powers must contain the identity element (or the neutral element).	J, J^2, J^3, J^4 J U J U
Fourth Theorem	In every such cycle of powers there must occur an inverse for every element.	Since in the cycle of powers J^2 and J^4 are equal to U, and since the example for the Fourth Postulate has an element as its own inverse, then J and J^3 must be the inverse of the element J in this cycle of powers.
Fifth Theorem	If one starts with any element of any finite group, and forms the set of all its powers, this set will satisfy all the group postulates and will, therefore, form a group.	From the examples for the First, Second and Third Theorems it is evident that any element as a base will form a subgroup consisting of that element and the element U.

Figure 4.1. Four basic postulates and eight theorems illustrated by examples from Table 4.1.

Postulate or Theorem:	Statement of the Postulate or Theorem of Group Theory:	Example Taken From Table 4.1 Table:
Sixth Theorem	The order of each subgroup is a divisor of the order of the parent group.	The elements J and U form a subgroup of order 2. This is a subgroup of the parent group of order 16. Since 2 is a divisor of 16, Theorem 6 applies.
Seventh Theorem	For any positive integer $\underline{n}$, there exists one and only one cyclic group of order $\underline{n}$.	Since, by definition, a group or subgroup, all of whose elements occur in the sequence of the powers of some single element, is a cyclic group or a cyclic subgroup; $\underline{and}$ since the subgroup J and U (order 2) is such a subgroup; $\underline{then}$ this is the basic and only cyclic subgroup of order 2. All other cyclic subgroups of Order 2 will be, in fact, isomorphic.
Eighth Theorem	If the order of a group is a prime number, then only one group exists, namely the cyclic group for the given order.	Since the group of order 16 does not have an order that is a prime number, then a cyclic group and one or more non-cyclic groups of order 16 may exist. By the definition of a cyclic group in the Seventh Theorem the parent group of order 16 is $\underline{not}$ a cyclic group.
$\underline{Principle}$	Every finite group of any kind is isomorphic with some one of the so-called permutation groups.	The order of the parent group, 16, is a divisor of 720 (or 6!), and so must be isomorphic to a subgroup of order 16 of the permutation group for 6 items.

Figure 4.1 Continued.

structure of <u>any</u> group that would be isomorphic with that specific parent group of Order 16. These generalizations, for instance, do <u>not</u> depend upon the specific elements that in Table 4.1 exhibit what has been called pairedness. Any two elements that can exhibit pairedness could, theoretically, form such a pair and, if their interactions with the other elements in the group met the requirements of the pattern of Table 4.2, they would be satisfactory substitutes for the pairs specifically found in Table 4.1.

CONSTRUCTING AN ISOMORPHIC ABSTRACT GROUP

If one accepts the apparently reasonable proposition that what is reported in Tables 3.1 and 3.2 is also represented in Tables 4.1 and 4.2, then one may ask what kind of group is represented by these various interaction tables. This question leads naturally to the question of whether, in fact, these groups are mathematical groups at all. One can identify four basic postulates of group theory (Denbow and Goedicke, 1959). These postulates also are referred to as the basic properties of a mathematical group. Part of an answer to the question of what kind of a group is represented by Tables 3.1, 3.2, 4.1, and 4.2 can be discovered by asking if it is possible to illustrate the basic properties of a mathematical group from the interaction tables of those four Tables. In Figure 4.1, examples from Table 4.1 are used to illustrate not only the four basic postulates but also an additional set of eight theorems derived from them as statements that further define a mathematical group (Denbow and Goedicke, 1959).

As can be seen, the specific interactions posited in Tables 3.1, 3.2 and 4.1 readily illustrate not only these four basic postulates but, as well, the eight listed theorems. Thus, the group of interactions posited in these three Tables form, in fact, a mathematical group. This group's interactions exhibit closure, the property of associativity, a neutral or identity element, and an inverse (although, in this group, each element in the set of elements functions as a self-inverse).

To determine whether the mathematical group that is displayed in Tables 3.1, 3.2 and 4.1 is Abelian involves asking whether commutativity can be illustrated from the several interaction tables. This question of commutativity is equivalent to asking whether for any three elements x, y and z, a commutative relationship exists in terms of these interaction tables. It all comes down to three questions: e.g.,

Q. 1   Is it true that $xy = z = yx$?
Q. 2   Is it true that $xz = y = zx$?
Q. 3   Is it true that $yz = x = zy$?

If these three questions can be answered affirmatively from the interaction tables of Tables 3.1, 3.2, or 4.1, the group displayed in those tables is commutative and, so, deserves the appellation of Abelian.

If one chooses any two elements from the margins of the tables of Tables 3.1, 3.2 or 4.1 such that the two elements chosen are not identical (i.e., so that $x \neq y$), and then lets the column-row intersection for those two elements define the third element (i.e., $xy = z$), then the three equivalences listed above as Q.1, Q.2 and Q.3 should hold true, if the group is in fact Abelian. While the reader can easily perform this exercise, let us suppose that the x is the element $\underline{S}$, the y the element $\underline{R}$ and the table used is that in Table 4.1. Then the column-row intersection for column $\underline{S}$ and row $\underline{R}$ is the element $\underline{L}$, which should be the z element. The three questions, then, affirm the following relationships, if a commutative property characterizes this particular group.

1. Is it true that $xy = z = yx$? This is the same as affirming that $S*R = L = R*S$. If we let the first-position be the column and the second-position be the row, and if we let the third term between the equal signs be the column-row intersection, this question is: Is it true that S(column) and R(row) have L as their column-row intersection? And is it true that R(column) and S(row) also have L as their column-row intersection? Inspection of Table 4.1 indicates that this is true in both instances.

2. Is it true that $xz = y = zx$? This is the same as affirming that $S*L = R = L*S$. Using the same conventions as were used previously, inspection of Table 4.1 indicates that this also is true.

3. Is it true that $yz = x = zy$? This is the same as affirming that $R*L = S = L*R$. Again, using the same convention used in the first example, inspection of Table 4.1 indicates this is true.

Therefore, one can conclude that the group of Order 16 displayed in Tables 3.1, 3.2 and 4.1 is commutative or Abelian. Since we also have seen that the group displayed in Table 4.2 is equivalent to the group that is displayed in Tables 3.1, 3.2 and 4.1, the group in Table 4.2 is also Abelian. Thus, the group displayed in each of these Tables is an Abelian group in which each element exhibits the property of being its own inverse.

The order apparent in Table 4.2 appears to be maximum and inherent and to be associated with this particular Abelian group of Order 16. However, one could still wonder whether some way could exist to construct an abstract mathematical group that would be isomorphic to the one that is displayed in Table 4.2. If this construct could be done, it would be possible to learn even more about the nature of the actual group affirmed in these first four figures. In all probability, such findings also would specify further the nature of the group structure being proposed as a model of human personality. That is, if some set of general principles exists whereby one can construct an abstract group isomorphic to the group of Table 4.2, then what is an intriguing fact would also represent a set of general principles which would be a better and stronger description of the nature of the model we wish to propose.

The attempt to construct such an abstract group is, in fact, not so difficult. In a short little book entitled Graphs, Groups and Games the late Augustus H. Fox provided an illustration of an abstract group that was Abelian but not cyclic. The group was formed by two "generators," a and b, which had two properties: (1) $a^2 = I = b^2$, and (2) $ab = ba$ (Fox, 1970). Fox called that group "the four group." He indicated that this group could be regarded as having been formed from a normally cyclic group generated by a and I and another cyclic group generated by b and I: that is, two cyclic groups of Order 2. Fox also noted that this was the same as saying that the group was the Cartesian product of the two groups of Order 2.

The table for Fox's four group is of considerable interest, for it appears to be isomorphic with the pattern of interactions that was discerned in Table 4.2 for the interactions of the four sets of four elements each. Moreover, this pattern of interactions also is isomorphic with the pattern of interactions among the four elements of the so-called "Uniqueness Elements" set (see the fifth generalization listed previously). In Fox's notation, the non-cyclic group generated as the Cartesian product of two groups of Order 2, in which each element functioned as its own inverse and in which the property of commutativity was exhibited, had an interaction table that looks like Table 4.3.

By a simple symbol substitution convention, (i.e., let ab = c), the equivalence between the "four group" and the pattern and regularity that the fifth generalization identified in the group of Order 16 is obvious. Given the conclusions reached above, this order is implicit in the group interaction tables displayed in Tables 3.1, 3.2, 4.1, and 4.2. Moreover, this isomorphism suggests that one should be able to construct abstract groups of orders higher than Order 4 using the basic "four group" procedure. That is, the possibility exists to construct abstract groups that are Abelian by using the same properties as Fox's "four group" and a number of generators

Table 4.3. An Abelian Group Generated as the Cartesian Product
of Two Cyclic Groups of Order 2 Using the Self-
Inverse.

	I	a	b	ab
I	I	a	b	ab
a	a	I	ab	b
b	b	ab	I	a
ab	ab	b	a	I

equal to the exponent of 2 that would give the total number of
group elements.

For example, a group of Order 8 should require three generators, since 8 is 2 raised to the third power. Similarly,
the possibility exists to create a group of Order 16 using four
generators, since 16 is 2 raised to the fourth power. Also the
possibility exists to speak of a group of Order 8 as the Cartesian product of three cyclic groups of Order 2 (e.g., groups
formed by I and a, I and b, and I and c). Or it should be possible to speak of a group of Order 16 as the Cartesian product
of four cyclic groups of Order 2. Moreover, the resulting
groups should be isomorphic with the group displayed in Table
4.2. If this be so, then Fox's procedure would seem to be the
most parsimonious way of describing the basic inherent nature
of the group structure of the group of Order 16 displayed in
Tables 3.1, 3.2, 4.1, and 4.2.

Experience indicates that, in fact, one can construct an
abstract group of Order 16 using Fox's procedure. If one posits four generators (e.g., a, b, c, and d) and also posits that
each is its own inverse (e.g., $a^2 = I = b^2 = I = c^2 = I = d^2$)
and, finally, that the group is commutative (e.g., ab = ba,
ac = ca, ad = da, bc = cb, bd = db, and cd = dc), then an
Abelian group of Order 16 can be created that will be isomorphic to the group displayed in Table 4.2. The table for such
an abstract group of Order 16 is displayed in Table 4.4, along
with a set of symbol substitution conventions that make the
isomorphism between Table 4.4 and Table 4.2 obvious.

When these simple, straightforward symbol equivalences are
used, the interaction table in Table 4.4 becomes the interaction table in Table 4.2. Thus, the one-to-one correspondence
requisite for an isomorphism is satisfied. Implicitly, then,

Table 4.4. An Abstract Abelian Group's Interaction Table.

	1 I	2 a	3 b	4 ab	5 c	6 ac	7 bc	8 abc	9 d	10 ad	11 bd	12 abd	13 cd	14 acd	15 bcd	16 abcd
I	I	a	b	ab	c	ac	bc	abc	d	ad	bd	abd	cd	acd	bcd	abcd
a	a	I	ab	b	ac	c	abc	bc	ad	d	abd	bd	acd	cd	abcd	bcd
b	b	ab	I	a	bc	abc	c	ac	bd	abd	d	ad	bcd	abcd	cd	acd
ab	ab	b	a	I	abc	bc	ac	c	abd	bd	ad	d	abcd	bcd	acd	cd
c	c	ac	bc	abc	I	a	b	ab	cd	acd	bcd	abcd	d	ad	bd	abd
ac	ac	c	abc	bc	a	I	ab	b	acd	cd	abcd	bcd	ad	d	abd	bd
bc	bc	abc	c	ac	b	ab	I	a	bcd	abcd	cd	acd	bd	abd	d	ad
abc	abc	bc	ac	c	ab	b	a	I	abcd	bcd	acd	cd	abd	bd	ad	d
d	d	ad	bd	abd	cd	acd	bcd	abcd	I	a	b	ab	c	ac	bc	abc
ad	ad	d	abd	bd	acd	cd	abcd	bcd	a	I	ab	b	ac	c	abc	bc
bd	bd	abd	d	ad	bcd	abcd	cd	acd	b	ab	I	a	bc	abc	c	ac
abd	abd	bd	ad	d	abcd	bcd	acd	cd	ab	b	a	I	abc	bc	ac	c
cd	cd	acd	bcd	abcd	d	ad	bd	abd	c	ac	bc	abc	I	a	b	ab
acd	acd	cd	abcd	bcd	ad	d	abd	bd	ac	c	abc	bc	a	I	ab	b
bcd	bcd	abcd	cd	acd	bd	abd	d	ad	bc	abc	c	ac	b	ab	I	a
abcd	abcd	bcd	acd	cd	abd	bd	ad	d	abc	bc	ac	c	ab	b	a	I

	1	2	3	4	5	6	7	8	9	10	11	12	13	14	15	16
I	I	a	b	ab	c	ac	bc	abc	d	ad	bd	abd	cd	acd	bcd	abcd
l	l	a	b	c	d	e	f	g	h	i	j	k	l	m	n	o

104

the parent group of Order 16 displayed in Tables 3.1, 3.2, and 4.1 also is described by the principles used to generate the abstract group of Table 4.4. The goal of a general description of the group structure model of personality, it seems, has been reached. One can understand mathematically the nature of the posited interactions. With this accomplishment, possibly one can look at the specifics of the group affirmed by Table 3.1 and, thereby, ask and decide some basic questions about the group structure model of personality.

ANALYZING THE PARENT GROUP USING THE ABSTRACT GROUP

Since the interaction tables displayed in Tables 4.1, 4.2, and 4.4 are isomorphic, it seems reasonable to hold that the principles used to construct the abstract group also hold for the specific group affirmed by Table 4.1. That is, we should be able to set up a series of symbol substitution conventions that would equate the specific elements of Table 4.1 with the elements symbolized in Table 4.4. Such a set of conventions would look like Figure 4.2, where four columns put into evident relationship the abstract group element symbol (i.e., a lower case letter), the original element symbol (i.e., an upper case letter), the original element Title taken from Table 3.1, and the original assignment of an element to a particular set of four elements, also taken from Table 3.1.

From Figure 4.2 it is obvious that, taking the marginal sequence used in Table 4.1 as a standard, the abstract group posits certain very fundamental affirmations about the nature of the elements in the specific group of Table 4.2. For example, the marginal sequencing and symbol substitution conventions used imply that the elements symbolized by the upper case letters S, E, R and W are the basic generating elements for the group of Order 16. The implication is equally clear that each of the other elements represents a certain uniquely complex relationship between two or more of the four generator elements.

The use of the abstract group assists one in asking and discovering an answer to the basic question of whether the marginal order of elements posited in Table 4.1 is either the best or the correct order. One can also ask if any other possible order could yield an equally obvious isomorphism. Specifically, one can ask whether there could be another (or other) marginal sequence that would produce a generalized table identical to that displayed in Table 4.2. This question is natural and, of course, vital if the group structure is to serve as a model of personality _per se_.

Manipulation of marginal sequencing of elements has indicated that, in fact, the sequence used in Table 4.1 is _not_ the

Abstract Group in Table 4.4	Specific Group in Table 4.1	Original Element Titles (See Table 3.1)	Original Set of Four Elements in Table 3.1
I	U	Uniqueness	"Uniqueness"
a	S	Self-desires & Drive	"Uniqueness"
b	E	Endowment Resources	"Uniqueness"
ab	V	Vision of Destiny	"Uniqueness"
c	R	Roles Played toward Destiny	"Short-term"
ac	L	Learning Potential & Skills	"Short-term"
bc	H	Home Laboratory Potentials	"Short-term"
abc	D	Decision-Making Skills	"Short-term"
d	W	Perceived Situation of One's Broadening World	"Long-term"
ad	P	Philosophy of Values	"Long-term"
bd	M	Measurement of Character Potentials	"Long-term"
abd	X	Personality Methods of Evaluation	"Long-term"
cd	C	Courage to Strive toward Maximum Potential	"Motivational"
acd	A	Action-investment of Energy toward Destiny	"Motivational"
bcd	J	Judgment and Wisdom	"Motivational"
abcd	G	Maturity of Growth Potentials	"Motivational"

Figure 4.2. Symbol substitution conventions contributing to isomorphism.

106

only possible one. Minimally, there are several other sequences that do not lose the advantage of highlighting the maximum inherent order within the group of Order 16. One can sequence elements along the margin several ways and still generate a table isomorphic to those displayed in Tables 4.2 and 4.4. Thus, the marginal sequence in Table 4.1 is neither the only possible one nor, necessarily, the best possible one.

What we have just affirmed is that the group structure model has sufficient flexibility to require use of some criterion or criteria for the best possible ordering of the marginal sequence. The differences between Tables 3.1 and 3.2 suggest that, originally, Ligon did not have any such criterion or criteria, while recourse to his published descriptions indicates that he did not address himself to this question at all (Ligon, 1969, 1970). Therefore, there does not exist in the history of the discovery and development of this particular group of Order 16 a rationale for the marginal sequencing of the elements. However, that lack of rationale need not imply that the elements represent no rationale or that the pattern of inter-element interactions is not discernible. The lack of an identified rationale does permit resequencing of elements along the margin in terms of varied criteria and judging results initially in terms of face validity by comparison with the abstract group of Table 4.4. The situation also permits one to offer refined definitional statements for each of the several elements of the group of Order 16.

The problem of a criterion for the marginal sequence occupied one of us for well over twelve months. During that period we tried out a number of possible sequences, and discovered successively the generalizations we have listed previously. Finally, because the model seemed a useful way of describing developmental processes, (at least in cross-section), we began to investigate the possibility of using a developmental/genetic sequence as the criterion for the marginal sequence.

The observation that one could allow the interactions of the set of four so-called "Uniqueness Elements" (i.e., the elements symbolized as U, S, E and V) with the first-position elements in each of the other three sets of four elements to determine the intra-set sequence in each of those other three sets suggested that it would be most important to apply the criterion of a developmental/genetic sequence to the four elements of the "Uniqueness Elements" set. This we did, investigating each of the logically possible sequences before we chose an intra-set order.

In terms of the set of four elements identified as the "Uniqueness Elements," the following considerations were involved in our seeking a developmental/genetic sequence. First,

as a matter of sheer logical or chronological priority, we
asked which of the four elements was the most obviously "first"
in any sequence. It seemed that the element U was most obviously a "first" element. U seemed to be so because it functioned as the identity (or neutral) element in the group and,
so, was in the first place, according to the model of the abstract group. It also seemed deserving of a first-position because, under any rational ordering, "uniqueness" seemed like a
fundamental or "first" concept. Therefore, the element U was
assigned the first-position within the set of four "Uniqueness
Elements."

Ordering of the remaining three elements in the "Uniqueness
Elements" set did not have quite the same sense of obviousness.
However, the concept of a genetic sequence suggested that the
question really was fundamentally an empirical or chronological
question: Which element is most likely to be evident and/or
formed next? and which next? and which next? A consideration
of the various possible sequences suggested that element E,
which related to generic endowments, should follow the more
philosophically posited "first" of element U. This choice reduced possibilities for a third-position to the elements S and
V. Considering the suggestive titling in Table 3.1 and Figure
4.2, it seemed that element S, which involved one's Self-Image,
including one's self-related desires and drives, was in all
likelihood a more obvious "next" than element V, which implied a future orientation needed for a "vision" of one's "destiny" or future. Thus, by applying a general developmental/
genetic criterion to the four elements in the so-called
"Uniqueness Elements" set of Table 3.1, we were led to conclude
that a criterion-determined sequence of elements would be U, E,
S and V.

Next, we considered whether it was necessary to maintain
the marginal sequence of the four sets of four elements exhibited in Table 3.1. This consideration resolved itself into the
question of whether it was possible to shift the marginal sequence of sets and still create an interaction table isomorphic
with the table of either Table 4.2 or 4.4. Sheer experimentation indicated that the sequence of the sets of four elements
was not inherent to the structure of the group of Order 16 displayed in Table 3.1. In fact, we found that it was possible to
create isomorphic interaction tables with differing set-
sequences. This discovery led us to ask which pair of sets
made most sense, considering that (a) we were attempting to
identify an over-all sequence based on a developmental/genetic
criterion, and (b) the abstract group's interaction table indicated that the parent group had an ordered interaction of two
sets of eight elements each. This led to the question of which
of the other sets of elements was most like the "Uniqueness
Elements" set, which was accepted as the standard abstract

group for determining the sequencing of the other three sets. We chose to match the "Uniqueness Elements" set with the so-called "Motivational Elements" set, which consisted of the elements symbolized as C, A, J and G. We made this choice because it seemed that both the "Uniqueness Elements" and the "Motivational Elements" sets consisted of elements that were more strongly individual-related than were the elements in the other two sets. The elements in the "Short-term Elements" and the "Long-term Elements" sets seemed to be more extra-individual related, especially when they were compared to the other set of eight elements. Thus, we decided to put the "Motivational Elements" set of four elements into a second set-sequential position along the margin.

The next decision involved determination of the most appropriate set-sequence for the so-called "Short-term Elements" and the "Long-term Elements" sets. Our choice was made after we considered our criterion and recognized (a) that the "Short-term Elements" set seemed somewhat more obviously individual-related than the "Long-term Elements" set, especially when the suggestive titles were considered, and (b) the criterion seemed to suggest that short-term effects were more likely to appear earlier than the long-term effects in the process of human development. Thus, we chose to put the "Short-term Elements" into a third set-sequential position and leave the "Long-term Elements" set in the fourth position along the margin of the interaction table.

We now had a set-sequential marginal ordering which, through experimentation, we discovered could be used to create an interaction table isomorphic to the tables displayed in Tables 4.1, 4.2, and 4.4. However, we now faced yet another series of choices, for the procedures listed earlier as seven basic generalizations suggested that several intra-set sequences could lead to interaction tables that would be isomorphic to our standard abstract group, the "uniqueness set." The question involved choosing the element in each of the remaining three sets of four elements which best functioned in a first-position within the set and which, across sets, best combined with two other first-position elements, in accord with the developmental/genetic criterion we were using. We chose to resolve this question a set at a time, recognizing that after the question had been answered for the second and third sets, an answer for the fourth set of elements would follow as a natural consequence.

Therefore, we first applied the criterion of developmental/genetic priority to the four elements in the "Motivational Elements" set. We tried several possible sequences, but finally concluded that although each of the several elements had to be understood in reference to "mature" capabilities, each also had prototypical or developmental predecessor capabilities that had to be considered. This conclusion led us to suspect that element A, understood at a prototypical level as action or motion, was a best candidate for the first-position spot in this intra-set sequence. Once made, this decision could then be applied to the rest of the intra-set sequence by studying its interaction with the four elements of the "Uniqueness Elements" set. This resultant sequence had an almost surprising reasonableness about it, for the intra-set sequence of the four elements in the "Motivational Elements" set turned out to be A, G, C and J. As we considered the result, it seemed increasingly likely that "action" or motion preceded "growth," and that both preceded "courage" or persistence, while all three preceded "judgment" or "wisdom." Thus, we settled upon this intra-set sequence for the "Motivational Elements."

We next asked about the developmental/genetic priority of the four elements in the "Short-term Elements" set. We discovered that this gave us a somewhat more complex choice, for the element placed into the first-position in this set would, through interaction with element A, determine the first-position element within the "Long-term Elements" set. Thus, we considered both the developmental/genetic firstness of each element and, as well, the effect of a choice of each element upon the intra-set sequence for the "Long-term Elements" set.

Finally, we concluded that the element D, understood as simple choice (a prototypical capability for the more "mature" capability of decision-making), seemed to be the best all-around candidate for the first-position in the "Short-term Elements" set. That choice determined the intra-set sequence through the interaction of element D with the four elements in the "Uniqueness Elements" set. Our determined sequence was, then, D, L, H and R. Again, reflection indicated a surprising reasonableness about this sequence. That is, it seemed likely that when thinking genetically and/or developmentally, "choice" preceded "learning," that both preceded recognition and use of "resources," and that all three preceded appearance of "roles." The sequence within the "Short-term Elements" set seemed to us to have a certain face validity that we found hard to ignore, so we settled upon it.

The choices we have recorded so far for three of the four sets of four elements determined both the first-position element in the intra-set sequence for the fourth "Long-term Elements" set and, thereby, the whole intra-set sequence of elements. The sequence of elements determined for the fourth set was M, W, X, and P. Consideration of both the abstract group symbol equivalences (Table 4.4) and the possible prototypical capabilities convinced us of a need for a clearer statement of element definitions for each of the elements in the parent group of Order 16. However, also evident was that if the elements M and W were to be associated as a pair, then both had to have something to do with an individual's "world," and that element M had to be developmentally prior to element W. In much the same way, it became clear that if X and P were to be a pair, then the prototypical capability of "evaluating" was developmentally prior to the formalization and systematization implied by "philosophy." Moreover, consideration of the abstract group symbol equivalences for these marginal positions suggested that it was sensible to regard "philosophy" as a synthesizing activity of the group-generator elements E, S, A and D. Therefore, on the basis of our prior decisions to put elements A and D into first-position in each of their respective sets of four elements, we settled upon the marginal sequence for the "Long-term Elements."

The symbol substitution conventions for our newly sequenced marginal positions and the general abstract group of Table 4.4 are given in Figure 4.3. These conventions indicate that, in a newly sequenced group of Order 16, the elements E, S, A and D function as generators for an Abelian group. Reflection suggested that this idea had a kind of sense to it, which we did not want to ignore.

The symbol substitutions suggested in Figure 4.3, which identify the four elements E, S, A and D as the generators in this Abelian group, can lead to several interesting and possibly useful affirmations. If these four generator elements were taken as representatives of kinds or classes of variables presumedly influencing human personality, then this marginal sequencing and set of symbol substitution conventions seem equivalent to the following five affirmations:

First, personality is a function of a human's genetic endowments or heredity.

Second, human personality is a function of a distinctly individual perception (i.e., the element S).

Third, human personality is a function of an individual's "activity" (i.e., the element A).

Fourth, human personality is a function of a set of individual "choices" (i.e., the element D).

Fifth, what we know as personality is the result of a complex, multiplicative interaction of these four generator elements and a set of other elements created as a result of that interaction.

Abstract Group in Table 4.4:	Specific Group in Table 4.1:	Original Element Titles (See Table 3.1)	Original Set of Four Elements in Table 3.1:
I	U	Uniqueness	"Uniqueness"
a	E	Endowments	"Uniqueness"
b	S	Self-desires & Self-drives	"Uniqueness"
ab	V	Vision (of destiny)	"Uniqueness"
c	A	Action Investment	"Motivational"
ac	G	Growth	"Motivational"
bc	C	Courage	"Motivational"
abc	J	Judgment	"Motivational"
d	D	Decision-Making	"Short-term"
ad	L	Learning	"Short-term"
bd	H	Home Resources	"Short-term"
abd	R	Roles Played	"Short-term"
cd	M	Measurement of Character	"Long-term"
acd	W	World (perceived)	"Long-term"
bcd	X	Evaluation (methods of)	"Long-term"
abcd	P	Philosophy (of values)	"Long-term"

Figure 4.3. Revised set of symbol substitution conventions.

These five affirmations seem to us to be a way of affirming that human personality itself is both complex and dynamic and, therefore, very like a system.

The symbol substitution conventions of Figure 4.3 suggest, again, the need for definitional statements for each of the group elements. This need has probably been evident for some time, but the attempt to discover and use a criterion for marginal sequencing made that need more obvious. Recognition of the existence of both a prototypical and a mature level of meaning for each of these elements also made that need evident. Moreover, the symbol substitutions proposed for the newly resequenced group of Order 16 suggested to us a way to begin to think rationally about such definitional statements. We undertook to supply such definitions out of a general conviction that definition was necessary, and out of a sense that our work has led us to some conclusions about the nature of the elements in this group.

What we have been able to accomplish in the way of definitional statements is the result of two convictions. First, we are convinced of the need to define each element in the group structure we have been considering. Second, we are convinced of a need to move toward the ability to "measure" each of these posited elements of human personality, and we know that definitions are needed if that measuring is to be done. In the next section we propose a definition for each element in our marginally resequenced parent group of Order 16. These statements represent multiply revised statements that began with our concern for "measurement" but which are still insufficiently defined or tested operationally to permit ready translation into "measurement" terms. Although the statements seem, at this point, to conform to our perceptions of the genesis and the future of our group, they can serve only as hopeful signs that point us and others toward effective "measurement" of human personality. The proposals advance this possibility by approaching the task in terms of variables that are more commonly considered in theories of human personality than are those derived from titles found in Table 3.1

DEFINING THE ELEMENTS IN THE GROUP

The following sixteen definitional statements are a way of moving toward four desired goals. First, they offer more substantial meaning to the group of elements that, up to this point, we have dealt with from a quite theoretical and abstract point of view. Second, they seem to suggest measurement in a way that some of the original element titles did not. Third, they are a means of further elucidating the group structure as a model of individual personality. Fourth, they implicitly suggest a model of personality research that seems to us less distorting and less limiting of human possibilities. We trust that the reader will discern a movement toward these goals in what follows.

The Identity Element: UNIQUENESS.

UNIQUENESS is a philosophically posited attribute that is presumed to be present from the moment of conception.

N.B.: Within the parent group of Order 16 the element symbolized by the letters U and I functions as a neutral or identity element. UNIQUENESS is a holistic concept that includes the idea of similarity yet recognizes the existence of difference, making it logically impossible to posit exact equivalence. UNIQUENESS involves a more precise recognition of the full implication of "individual difference."

The First Generator: ENDOWMENTS.

ENDOWMENTS are what an individual can, in fact, "do" at any given moment.

N.B.: Within the parent group of Order 16 the element symbolized by the letters E and a functions as a "first" of several generator elements. ENDOWMENTS include both genetically controlled attributes (i.e., things that may be regarded as inherited) and environmentally controlled abilities (i.e., things that may be regarded as learned, as distinct from inherited). This element is a genotypical concept that is inferred from phenotypical behavior.

The Second Generator: SELF-IMAGE.

SELF-IMAGE is the "picture" an individual has of himself or herself as a total personality.

N.B.: Within the parent group of Order 16 the element symbolized by the letters S and b functions as a "second" of several generator elements. SELF-IMAGE is primarily a present-related concept. The construction of an image of the Self as distinct from its surrounding environment is a basic accomplishment of the period of Infancy. Upon that foundation one's present SELF-IMAGE has been successively re-constructed through the processes of differentiation, specification and generalization.

The Fourth Element: VISION.

VISION is an individually held, pervasive, goal-specific self-related intention.

N.B.: Within the parent group of Order 16 the element symbolized by the letters V and ab functions as a distinguishable "product" of the first and second generators. VISION is primarily a future-related concept. It serves an individual as a personal "sense of direction."

The Third Generator: ACTION.

ACTION is overt or observable behavior (i.e., activity), including a "willingness" to engage in such behavior.

N.B.: Within the parent group of Order 16 the element symbolized by the letters A and c functions as a "third" of several generator elements. ACTION is initially (during the period of Infancy) overt behavior; later it is such behavior when, as and if ACTION seems "relevant" to an individual's immediate and limited intentions. While ACTION is similar to physical movement, the concept includes a recognition of the function of present intention. ACTION is primarily a present-related concept.

The Sixth Element: GROWTH.

GROWTH is the degree to which a complex, genetically controlled range of possibilities is approximated.

N.B.: Within the parent group of Order 16 the element symbolized by the letters G and ac functions as a distinguishable "product" of the first and third generators. GROWTH tends to develop or "increase" with Chronological Age. Conceptually, it is similar to (but not identical to) the construct of a ratio Mental Age. Thus, GROWTH successively approximates a continually changing set of discernible possibilities.

The Seventh Element: COURAGE.

COURAGE is, basically, individual persistence.

N.B.: Within the parent group of Order 16 the element symbolized by the letters C and bc functions as a distinguishable "product" of the second and third generators. COURAGE is particularly readily recognizable as individual persistence "in the 'face' of" disapproval by individually relevant "others." Sheer, simple persistence "grows" (or "develops") into COURAGE as the nature and locus of the individually relevant "others" also changes across time (i.e., as the individual "grows" or "develops").

The Eighth Element: JUDGMENT.

JUDGMENT is the level of complexity of information one regards as relevant and/or "necessary," when called upon to choose one from among several "evident" courses of action.

N.B.: Within the parent group of Order 16 the element symbolized by the letters J and abc functions as a distinguishable "product" of the first, second and third generators. JUDGMENT apparently becomes "wise" as certain kinds of information are included within the realm of the "relevant" and, so, affect the post-choice congruence between intent and result. JUDGMENT "develops" as the level of information regarded as relevant or "necessary" comes progressively more complex.

The Fourth Generator: DECISION MAKING.

DECISION MAKING is basically (and initially) the action of choosing.

N.B.: Within the parent group of Order 16 the element symbolized by the letters D and d functions as a "fourth" of several generator elements. With the passage of time and the occurrence of "development" DECISION MAKING comes to include a set of skills in information-gathering and information-processing that contributes to one's sense of the preferability or correctness of a given choice from amongst a set of alternatives. To the degree that "information-gathering" and "information-processing" may be legitimately inferred from the "action of choosing," DECISION MAKING might be considered to be that set of skills which (across time) is "developed" as the preceding influence "determining" one's choices. DECISION MAKING (d) and JUDGMENT (abc) exist at the conceptual interface between a Person and his or her Environment: they are similar, but usefully distinguishable concepts.

The Tenth Element: LEARNING.

LEARNING is, basically, the ability to acquire and use "new" information and/or skills.

116

N.B.: Within the parent group of Order 16 the element
symbolized by the letters R and abd functions as a distinguishable "product" of the first, second and fourth gen-
Fundamentally, LEARNING concerns an "ability" to acquire
and use information and skills. Later in the human life-
span, LEARNING may also be considered to include that
which has already been acquired: i.e., the extent (and
content) of one's existing repertoire of either "information" or "skills."

The Eleventh Element: HOME RESOURCES.

HOME RESOURCES are what an individual perceives to be
available to him or her as a "resource" in his or her
"home."

N.B.: Within the parent group of Order 16 the element
symbolized by the letters H and bd functions as a distinguishable "product" of the second and fourth generators.
Fundamentally, HOME RESOURCES involves a "match" between
what objectively is available to one and what subjectively
is perceived to be available to one in the "home," wherever or whatever that may be for one. The ideas of quan-
tity and a quantitiative ratio are inescapably part of this
concept: (e.g., "pessimism") would be expressed by ratios
between .00 and 1.00, "realism" by a ratio of (or very
close to) 1.00, and "optimism" by ratioes somewhat in
excess of 1.00.

The Twelfth Element: ROLES.

ROLES are complex behavioral patterns that are relatively
consistent across considerable periods of time.

N.B.: Within the parent group of Order 16 the element
symbolized by the letters R and abd functions as a distinguishable "product" of the first, second and fourth generators. Early in the human life-span ROLES may be imposed upon one through the expectations of "others" via
the mechanism of conditioning. Later, ROLES may be self-
imposed (i.e., "chosen") through a process of "conscious
choice," although such "choices" may involve one in the
use of the mechanism of conditioning for the "purpose" of
achieving (or approximating) self-chosen goals.

117

The Thirteenth Element: MEASURES OF CHARACTER.

MEASURES OF CHARACTER are one's basic perceptions of one's own placement within the personally known World.

N.B.: Within the parent group of Order 16 the element symbolized by the letters M and cd functions as a distinguishable "product" of the third and fourth generators. The element MEASURES OF CHARACTER involves two basic perceptions: the "manner" in which one is "positioned" or "placed" vis-a-vis that personally known World, and the "locus" of that positioning or placement within the limits of that personally known World. One's "character" may be inferred to be influenced by this basic perception of one's own "placement within the personally known World."

The Fourteenth Element: WORLD.

WORLD is the societal environment outside the "narrow" limits of one's "home" (or surrogate home) and immediate "family."

N.B.: Within the parent group of Order 16 the element symbolized by the letters W and acd functions as a distinguishable "product" of the first, third and fourth generators. With the passage of time, the extent of one's WORLD tends to "increase," sometimes quite drastically. WORLD is similar to the concept of one's "societal environment," since such an environment may be either specific and concrete or quite general and abstract. Any measure of WORLD inevitably would need to express "extent."

The Fifteenth Element: EVALUATION.

EVALUATION is a set of available and used skills for comparing actuality to known and accepted standards.

N.B.: Within the parent group of Order 16 the element symbolized by the letters X and bcd functions as a distinguishable "product" of the second, third and fourth generators. EVALUATION involves both prior knowledge of and existential commitment to a particular set of skills (i.e., those that tend to encourage, support and facilitate the comparison of either the proposed or the actual to some standard, so that both similarities and dissimilarities may be recognized). In all probability, this element involves a high level of what Piaget calls formal operational thinking and E. A. Peel calls explainer thinking.

118

The Sixteenth Element: PHILOSOPHY.

PHILOSOPHY is a complex, organized system of thinking about principles and values, and about their relationship to experiential "reality."

N.B.: Within the parent group of Order 16 the element symbolized by the letters P and abcd functions as a distinguishable "product" of the first, second, third and fourth generators. As such, PHILOSOPHY provides a kind of integration of the basic generators. One's set of basic "values" constitutes a subsystem within PHILOSOPHY and, so, are recognized as an important component of an organized system of thought. PHILOSOPHY almost certainly involves Piaget's formal operational thinking, since the "items" are abstract principles and generalizations.

The implications of these sixteen statements for the actual "measurement" of individual elements in the parent group of Order 16 are reserved for a later time. First, we want to consider the group structure itself as a potentially useful model of human personality. It is to that task that we turn our attention in the next few chapters.

CHAPTER

5

THE PATTERN, NOT THE PIECES, IS IMPORTANT

In Chapter 4 the somewhat gutsy question--What the hell is going on here?--was interpreted as a pointed expression of the general evaluative question. In response to it, the maximum inherent order of a parent group of Order 16 was both identified and displayed. In addition, a procedure for generating an abstract mathematical group isomorphic with that maximally ordered parent group was identified. This isomorphism led to questions of element priority or intra-set marginal order. The criterion of a developmental/genetic sequence was then used to settle upon one of the several possible intra-set marginal orders. As a result, the group structure model of personality received an explicable order that created an interaction table that was isomorphic with the abstract mathematical group interaction table displayed in Table 4.4. In the present Chapter, we propose to examine some implications of this group structure model for personality and personality theory.

THE CRITERION-SEQUENCED GROUP AS A MODEL

An interaction table for the criterion-sequenced parent group of Order 16 is displayed in Table 5.1. Since a developmental/genetic sequence was applied as a criterion to both the intra-set marginal sequence and to the inter-set marginal sequence, this ordering represents a twofold use of the criterion. The resulting interaction table is, of course, isomorphic with the tables displayed in Tables 4.2 and 4.4.

Since none of the element interactions have been changed, Table 5.1 is equivalent to Tables 3.1 and 3.2, except that the maximum inherent order of the mathematical group structure for this particular parent group of Order 16 has been highlighted. Table 5.1 also includes a series of conventions which indicate how interaction tables isomorphic with those in Tables 4.2 and

Table 5.1.   A Re-Ordered and Re-Sequenced Interaction Table Based on a Developmental/Genetic Criterion.

	U	E	S	V	A	G	C	J	D	L	H	R	M	W	X	P
U	U	E	S	V	A	G	C	J	D	L	H	R	M	W	X	P
E	E	U	V	S	G	A	J	C	L	D	R	H	W	M	P	X
S	S	V	U	E	C	J	A	G	H	R	D	L	X	P	M	W
V	V	S	E	U	J	C	G	A	R	H	L	D	P	X	W	M
A	A	G	C	J	I	E	S	V	M	W	X	P	D	L	H	R
G	G	A	J	C	E	I	V	S	W	M	P	X	L	D	R	H
C	C	J	A	G	S	V	U	E	X	P	M	W	H	R	D	L
J	J	C	G	A	V	S	E	U	P	X	W	M	R	H	L	D
D	D	L	H	R	M	W	X	P	U	E	S	V	A	G	C	J
L	L	D	R	H	W	M	P	X	E	U	V	S	G	A	J	C
H	H	R	D	L	X	P	M	W	S	V	U	E	C	J	A	G
R	R	H	L	D	P	X	W	M	V	S	E	U	J	C	G	A
M	M	W	X	P	D	L	H	R	A	G	C	J	U	E	S	V
W	W	M	P	X	L	D	R	H	G	A	J	C	E	U	V	S
X	X	P	M	W	H	R	D	L	C	J	A	G	S	V	U	E
P	P	X	W	M	R	H	L	D	J	C	G	A	V	S	E	U

U	E	S	V	A	G	C	J	D	L	H	R	M	W	X	P
1	a	b	c	d	e	f	g	h	i	j	k	l	m	n	o
I	a	b	ab	c	ac	bc	$\frac{abc}{c}$	d	ad	bs	$\frac{ab}{d}$	cd	$\frac{ac}{d}$	$\frac{bc}{d}$	$\frac{ab}{cd}$
1	2	3	4	5	6	7	8	9	10	11	12	13	14	15	16

Pair 1'	Pair a'	Pair b'	Pair c'	Pair d'	Pair e'	Pair f'	Pair g'

Pair of pairs: 1"	Pair of pairs: a"	Pair of pairs: b"	Pair of pairs: c"

122

4.4 can be formed through a simple process of symbol substitution.

Moreover, identification of the phenomenon of pairs of elements, and of pairs of pairs of elements, in the bottom rows of Table 5.1 indicates symbol substitutions that create illustrations of the first, second, fourth and fifth of the seven generalizations listed in Chapter 4. It seems reasonable to assume, since the tables in Tables 5.1 and 4.2 are isomorphic, that all seven of these generalizations hold true. If that is so, then those generalizations also are true of this (or of any) criterion-sequenced group of Order 16 that is based on the assumptions used to create this particular group.

To assume that all of these generalizations hold for this (or any) criterion-sequenced group is equivalent to saying that the application of the developmental/genetic sequence criterion to the marginal order of elements has not influenced the basic pattern of a maximum inherent order in the original parent group of Order 16. This observation also suggests that order, pattern, and regularity are truly inherent in the group structure and, so, are independent of the nature of the specific elements composing the group. This generalization will prove useful in any further analysis of the implications of using this mathematical group structure as a model of human personality.

LEVELS OF CONSTRUCTS IMPLICIT IN THE STRUCTURE

If one makes the reasonable assumption that the seven generalizations of Chapter 4 apply to the criterion-sequenced group, then, through a process of successive pairings, one can discern a series of levels of groupness implicit in this particular Abelian group of Order 16. Moreover, the number of such levels appears to be related to the number of different sized subgroups positable from any parent group of Order 16. As the sixth theorem in Table 4.3 suggests, the number of constructs at each such level of groupness equals a number which is a divisor of the Order of the parent group. Thus, the existence of levels of groupness ranging from eight, four, and two constructs to a single construct suggests that these sets are possible subgroups of the parent group.

If the group of sixteen originally posited elements is taken as a baseline of specificity, then the other discernible levels of groupness seem to represent a conceptual movement from specificity toward generality. This observation suggests that the mathematical group structure model of personality, qua model, implies that a rich, full, and consistent theory of personality will inevitably involve a series of interrelated levels of generality. Moreover, the model also implies that the constructs within any given level of generality in such a model will interact, at that level, as if they constituted an Abelian group.

Such a structure of levels of generality is presented in Figure 5.1. In this figure the sixteen original element symbols (i.e., upper case letters) appear at the bottom of the figure, while the discernible levels of related constructs appear in successive rows above these baseline symbols. This structure of levels appears to constitute a hierarchy of interrelated constructs. While the titling and identification of each of these successively more general construct sets is important, that effort is deferred to the following chapter. At this point, it seems more important first to note and then to consider this hierarchical structure of concepts.

The hierarchy of constructs abstractly symbolized in Figure 5.1 appears to be inherent in the group of Order 16. The hierarchy seems to be a function of the group, qua group. Thus, by virtue of discerning (or, even, of merely introducing) a mathematical group as a model of personality, we have gained a powerful conceptual and analytical device, the idea of a hierarchical series of levels of generality. This idea is analogous to the philosopher's device of specifying "levels of discourse." However, within this model the levels of generality have a certain specified interrelationship that, sometimes, philosophical "levels of discourse" do not seem to have.

For example, if one assumes that the sixteen original elements represent a baseline of relative specificity, then each of the four rows above that row represents related but more general levels of constructs. In the top row of Figure 5.1, therefore, one would expect to find the most general and inclusive construct in the model (e.g., the most general and inclusive construct in a theory of human personality). In the three intermediate rows, in a descending order of generality, one would expect to find constructs at three intermediate levels of generality. Each of these levels is related both to a level above it (more general) and to a level below it (more specific). It seems that we have a technique for conceptual discrimination of constructs that can contribute clarification and specification of a theory of personality and, so, to description of human personality per se.

Jean Piaget referred in Structuralism to the work of Kurt Godel to make the point that a structure similar to the multi-level hierarchical structure displayed in Figure 5.1 is useful. Piaget pointed out that Godel's work showed that the creation of a relatively rich and demonstrably consistent theory required more than simply the analysis of the theory's

Set of 16 Elements as One Set
(1'''')

Pair of Pair of Pairs
(Set of 8 Elements)
(1''')
.. .. ..

Pair of Pair of Pairs
(Set of 8 Elements)
(a''')
.. ..

Pair of Pairs
(Set of 4 Elements)
(1'')
.. ..

Pair of Pairs
(Set of 4 Elements)
(a'')
.. ..

Pair of Pairs
(Set of 4 Elements)
(b'')
.. ..

Pair of Pairs
(Set of 4 Elements)
(c'')
.. ..

Pair
(1')

Pair
(a')

Pair
(b')

Pair
(c')

Pair
(d')

Pair
(e')

Pair
(f')

Pair
(g')

$\frac{U}{1}$ $\frac{E}{a}$ $\frac{S}{b}$ $\frac{V}{c}$ $\frac{A}{d}$ $\frac{G}{e}$ $\frac{C}{f}$ $\frac{J}{g}$ $\frac{D}{h}$ $\frac{L}{i}$ $\frac{H}{j}$ $\frac{R}{k}$ $\frac{M}{l}$ $\frac{W}{m}$ $\frac{X}{n}$ $\frac{P}{o}$

$\overline{I}$ $\overline{a}$ $\overline{b}$ $\overline{ab}$ $\overline{c}$ $\overline{ac}$ $\overline{bc}$ $\overline{abc}$ $\overline{d}$ $\overline{ad}$ $\overline{bd}$ $\overline{abd}$ $\overline{cd}$ $\overline{acd}$ $\overline{bcd}$ $\overline{abcd}$

Figure 5.1. Hierarchically arranged levels implicit in the group.

125

presuppositions. According to Piaget, Godel showed that what was actually required was creation of a next higher theory. In theoretical structures, Godel showed the importance of a series of levels of theories or constructs. In fact, one must conclude that sheer simplicity is a _structural_ sign of _weakness_. To establish any explanation securely within the structure of human knowledge, Piaget noted, one must also create the next higher theory or explanation (Piaget, 1971).

We want to appropriate the concept that a thesis supported only by the simplicity associated with a limited number of constructs is weaker than one supported by the complexity associated with a greater number of hierarchically structured constructs. This thesis permits us to regard the series of interrelated levels of constructs in this group structure as an indication of strength and power. In addition, we also believe that Godel's work makes such a series of levels of generality both necessary and desirable. Naturally, we also recognize that Godel's thesis indicates that our group structure model must be presumed to exist within some even more extensive model.

The hierarchy of levels of generality posited in Figure 5.1 implies that the nature of the constructs at a given level of generality _can_ be and _must_ be identified through use of two complementary processes. For instance, one can imagine moving conceptually down from the construct at the most general level toward the specificity of the baseline. This downward movement implies a process of successive differentiation. Therefore, as one moves from a higher level of generality to a next lower level, one may expect that the number of restrictive conditions which characterize them will increase successively as the constructs are encountered. Since this group structure model involves a successive dichotomization of each construct, this downward movement could aptly be called a _minimizing differentiation_. The process requires successive identification of the parts that constitute the whole of the construct being differentiated. This process appears to be analogous to what usually is termed deduction.

The structure displayed in Figure 5.1 also implies that an opposite but complementary process does, or could exist in this model. Such a process would be one in which, successively, elements at a given level are grouped into pairs through a process of combination that might aptly be called dedifferentiation (Piaget, 1971). In this process the movement is upward from specificity toward increasing generality. In such an upward movement one encounters constructs at a next higher level that have fewer restrictive conditions characterizing them than did the constructs at the lower level. This process, then, identifies a more general whole to which the

126

pair of parts belongs. This whole is regarded conceptually as constituted by a relational operation between the two lower constructs. This process appears to be analogous to what usually is termed induction.

The hierarchically arranged series of levels of generality in Figure 5.1 implies that through mutually compatible processes of induction and deduction one can identify a series of constructs that form sets of constructs, all of which are parts of a model of human personality. The comments of Piaget and the work of Godel suggested that both processes are not only possible but necessary for an understanding of the constructs within such a group structure model. As we have seen, the nature of this particular group of Order 16 implies the same thing.

If the group structure we have presented is to be taken as a model of human personality (or of a theory of human personality), it becomes necessary to make a series of basic distinctions between constructs on the basis of their levels of generality. In addition, the model suggests that at each such level of generality the constructs at that level interact with one another as if they were elements in an Abelian group.

We began by attributing the properties of a mathematical group to a set of sixteen elements that were originally discerned simply as super clusters of research insights (Williams, 1970; Ligon, 1969, 1970). Now we can recognize that the group structure of the model insures that properties of a group inhere in sets of constructs that we had all too abstractly identified, and that processes of differentiation and dedifferentiation may be presumed to constitute these constructs. This does not presume, however, that as one moves between levels of generality the "constituting" and "constituted" constructs remain unchanged. It does affirm that such changed or transformed constructs preserve their recognizability and show some forms of invariance across levels (Piaget, 1971). The groupness of the constructs at each level of generality demonstrates that the whole hierarchically arranged model is pervasively an example of a mathematical group. That fact makes this model powerful. It also makes the problem of construct identification and titling important and its resolution possible.

CHAPTER **6**

SUBSTITUTING SYMBOLS FOR WORDS

The American folk-hero Bugs Bunny is famous for asking, "What's up, Doc?" At this point, that question is both real and useful. It can be interpreted as inquiring what we propose to call the constructs in the hierarchical series that is implicit in the group structure model. Rather than burden the reader with a long discussion of how we came to settle upon the titles, we will present the results of our thinking, look at the sometimes interesting results, and identify some ways in which the resulting structure seems to be heuristic. At the same time we will identify the possibilities that make this model for research one that is less distorting and less limiting than other constructs as well as being a paradigm for service and practice that is open to the complex interplay of forces that impinge formatively upon an individual. We believe the hierarchical structure implicit in the Abelian group of Order 16 that we have presented is a sensible response to Sanford's call for ". . . a paradigm . . . which respects the nature of man as a . . . creature who acts as well as behaves" (Sanford, 1970, p. x).

A HIERARCHY OF CONSTRUCTS: TITLES AND IMPLICATIONS

The implicit structure of levels constituting what we have called groupness has already been displayed in Figure 5.1. As we have noted, at each such level a set of constructs exists that functions as an Abelian group. Moreover, each level is related to every other level in a hierarchical structure that appears to parallel the continuum from specificity to generality. Therefore, we propose the series of construct titles that are displayed in Figure 6.1.

The hierarchy of constructs displayed in Figure 6.1 locates the most general and most inclusive construct in its Level I, and provides the title Personality. While this may

CONSTRUCTS

Level								
I	PERSONALITY (1'''')							
II	PERSON (1''')				ENVIRONMENT (a''')			
III	SELF (1'')		BEHAVIOR (a'')		FUNCTION (b'')		FIELD (c'')	
IV	ORGANISM (1')	PURPOSE (a')	ACTIVITY (b')	PERSISTENCE (c')	KNOWLEDGE (d')	EXPERIENCE (e')	SOCIETY (f')	VALUES (g')
V	U (1) E (a)	S (b) V (c)	A (d) G (e)	C (f) J (g)	D (h) L (i)	H (j) R (k)	M (l) W (m)	X (n) P (o)
ABSTRACT MATH GRP	I a	b ab	c ac	bc abc	d ad	bd abd	cd acd	bcd abcd
	The Uniqueness Set of Four "Elements"		The Motivational Set of Four "Elements"		The Short-term Set of Four "Elements"		The Long-term Set of Four "Elements"	

Figure 6.1. Titles for a hierarchical structure of personality.

seem like belaboring the obvious, a model of personality (or a model of a theory of personality) should have "personality" as its most inclusive, most general construct. However, the group structure model identifies this general construct with a total set of constituting elements or constructs, so that the generality and the inclusiveness have a series of increasingly specific references.

We identify the two constructs at Level II as _Person_ and _Environment_. These titles seem amenable to either an inductive or a deductive justification. That is, considering the two sets of eight elements at Level V that are summarized by the two general constructs Person and Environment, these titles seem apt generalities. Similarly, Personality _qua_ personality seems minimally to involve a person in a "setting" or environment and, so, to require such a titling. Of course, this titling suggests a not-so-new idea: one's personality is the result of, or is constituted by the interaction of a Person with his or her Environment. Piaget's process of adaptation consists of just such an interaction, and it involves the complementary processes he calls assimilation and accommodation (Piaget, 1967; Piaget & Inhelder, 1969). As a general theoretical assertion, we feel comfortable with Piaget's position and regard our Level II titling as conformable to that theory.

The Level III constructs are titled _Self_, _Behavior_, _Function_ and _Field_. These titles seem apt when viewed as results of the inductive and the deductive approaches. That is, the Level III titles suggest that the Level II construct titled Person is constituted by a Self plus its Behavior. Another way of stating this idea could be to say that Level III affirms that a Person is a behaving Self. Similarly, Level III affirms that the Level II construct Environment involved in constituting a Personality is, itself, constituted by (or analyzable into) two constructs, Function and Field. These rather general terms assume more specific meaning when it is realized that within the hierarchical structure they are, in turn, defined by levels above and below the level on which they appear.

In addition, Level III suggests that the interaction of Self, Behavior, Function and Field constitute Personality _per se_. If one uses the philosophical analog of levels of discourse, the group structure model suggests that consideration of the Self and its Behavior is, for Personality constitution, incomplete without consideration of Function (e.g., asking "functional" questions of "behavior") and Field (e.g., noting the context within which the Self behaves and, so, "functions"). The suggestion exists that through interaction of Behavior and Field one arrives at an understanding of Function; that through interaction of Function and Field one arrives at a description of Behavior; that through interaction of Behavior and Field one arrives at an insight into Function. These suggestions seem to be reasonable, and we regard that fact as an indication of the strength of the group structure model per se. In the terminology of research, there seems to be an isomorphism with experiential reality in these affirmations, and that is what is meant by the term validity.

When one recognizes Level IV, the number of constructs has grown to eight. These constructs represent both a next lower level from Level III and a next higher level from Level V. Thus, the titles proposed for Level IV represent constitutive constructs for the next higher level, as well as generalizations that are constituted by the constructs at the next lower level (i.e., the level of the original group of posited elements). For example, Self is affirmed to be constituted by the two constructs Organism and Purpose. Behavior also is affirmed to be constituted by the constructs Activity and Persistence. Function is affirmed to be constituted by the constructs Knowledge and Experience. Field is, finally, affirmed to be constituted by the constructs Society and Values.

The three interactions posited by the group structure model for Level III constructs also can be expressed in terms of Level IV constructs. Thus, the model's Abelian group suggests the three interactions, which can be expressed in terms of Level IV constructs.

Behavior Interacting with Function Leads to Field

This Level III interaction is equivalent to affirming that Activity and Persistence, as a set, interacting with Knowledge and Experience, as a set, lead to Society and Values, as a set. This seems equivalent to affirming that an understanding of the set consisting of Society and Values involves consideration of interactions of the sets consisting of Activity and Persistence and of Knowledge and Experience. This would seem to be analogous to affirming that Society and Values are resultants of a dynamic interaction created by the interfacing of individual activity and persistence with the seemingly cognitive construct Knowledge and the primarily cumulative, historical construct Experience.

Behavior Interacting with Field Leads to Function

This Level III interaction is equivalent to affirming that Activity and Persistence, as a set, interacting with Society and Values, as a set, lead to Knowledge and Experience, as a set. This idea seems equivalent to affirming that an understanding of the cognitive-historical set of Knowledge and Experience involves consideration of interactions of the sets consisting of Activity and Persistence and of Society and

Values. This also would seem to be analogous to affirming that Knowledge and Experience are resultants of a dynamic interaction created by the interfacing of individual activity and persistence with the societal constructs of Society and Values. This affirmation seems relatively unchallengeable.

Function Interacting with Field Leads to Behavior

This Level III interaction is equivalent to affirming that Knowledge and Experience, as a set, interacting with Society and Values, as a set, lead to Activity and Persistence, as a set. This process also seems equivalent to affirming that an understanding of individual Activity and Persistence involves consideration of interactions of the sets consisting of Knowledge and Experience and of Society and Values. This also would seem to be analogous to affirming that individual activity and persistence are the resultants of a dynamic interaction created by the interfacing of the cognitive-historical set composed of Knowledge and Experience with the societal set composed of Society and Values. Reflection upon this model-suggested interaction implies, in turn, that from activity and persistence one may move inferentially toward sets of cognitive-historical-societal constructs. Such a suggestion however may be but another way of affirming the need to consider context when seeking understanding of such individually related constructs as either Activity or Persistence. This affirmation, especially in this last form, seems relatively unchallengeable.

The example of these three translations of Level III interactions into Level IV constructs suggests that the group structure model has a strength that we find attractive. The model seems to dictate a series of relationships that appear to have the quality of being isomorphic with the reality encountered by many humans. That quality would seem to be a prerequisite for any model of personality, including this one.

FORMALIZING THE HIERARCHICAL STRUCTURE

The continued use of the full titles for the several constructs may prove to be cumbersome. Therefore, we propose a series of symbol conventions in Figure 6.2 that will enable us to specify inter-construct relationships in a more formal and elegant manner. Of course, these conventions are a matter of convenience. However, once these construct symbols are recognized, the hierarchical group structure can be quite succinctly stated.

The various interactions at Levels I, II, III and IV can be succinctly stated using these symbol conventions, plus three other symbols: one for the relation of interaction within a

Level V Symbols	Level IV Symbols	Level III Symbols	Level II Symbols	Level I Symbols

$$
\begin{array}{l}
\text{U} \\
\text{E} \\
\text{S} \\
\text{V}
\end{array}
\;-\;-\;-\;
\begin{array}{l}
\text{O}_{rg} \\
\text{P}_{rp}
\end{array}
\;-\;-\;
\text{S}_{lf}
\;-\;-\;\text{P}_{sn}
$$

$$
\begin{array}{l}
\text{A} \\
\text{G} \\
\text{C} \\
\text{J}
\end{array}
\;-\;-\;
\begin{array}{l}
\text{A}_{ct} \\
\text{P}_{st}
\end{array}
\;-\;-\;
\text{B}_{vr}
\;-\;-\;\text{P}_{ty}
$$

$$
\begin{array}{l}
\text{D} \\
\text{L} \\
\text{H} \\
\text{R}
\end{array}
\;-\;-\;
\begin{array}{l}
\text{K}_{nw} \\
\text{E}_{xp}
\end{array}
\;-\;-\;
\text{F}_{ct}
\;-\;-\;\text{E}_{vr}
$$

$$
\begin{array}{l}
\text{M} \\
\text{W} \\
\text{X} \\
\text{P}
\end{array}
\;-\;-\;
\begin{array}{l}
\text{S}_{ty} \\
\text{V}_{al}
\end{array}
\;-\;-\;
\text{F}_{ld}
$$

WHERE

O_{rg} = Organism	S_{lf} = Self	U, E, S, V,
P_{rp} = Purpose	B_{vr} = Behavior	A, G, C, J,
A_{ct} = Activity	F_{ct} = Function	D, L, H, R,
P_{st} = Persistence	F_{ld} = Field	M, W, X, P
K_{nw} = Knowledge	P_{sn} = Person	are Level V
E_{xp} = Experience	E_{vr} = Environment	elements, as
S_{ty} = Society	P_{ty} = Personality	defined in
V_{al} = Values		Chapter 4.

Figure 6.2. Symbols for a hierarchical structure of personality.

Level, another for the relation of constituting between Levels, and one for the _result_ of the interaction. If we let the symbol # stand for the relation of interaction within a _Level_, we will be able to write a series of intra-Level formulas. If we let the symbol + stand for the relation of _constituting_, we will be able to write another series of formulas for inter-Level relationships. Finally, if we let = stand for the _result_ of either an intra-Level interaction or an inter-Level constituting, we will be able to complete a third series of formulas. Although the symbols + and = are common mathematical symbols, in the formulas we will be proposing they are used without the full rigor of their common mathematical usage.

1. Level I Symbolic Formula

The only Level I formula would be:

$$P_{ty} \# P_{ty} = P_{ty}.$$

2. Level II Symbolic Formulas

At Level II one could write three formulas:

$$P_{sn} \# E_{vr} = E_{vr}; \quad E_{vr} \# E_{vr} = P_{sn}; \quad \text{and } P_{sn} \# P_{sn} = P_{sn}.$$

These formulas imply that P_{sn} functions within Level II as an identity or neutral element. The second and third formulas illustrate the self-inverse property for each of the two constructs found at Level II.

3. Level III Symbolic Formulas

At Level III the number of formulas that can be written increases. At this Level it is possible to write ten symbolic formulas:

$$S_{lf} \# B_{vr} = B_{vr}; \quad S_{lf} \# F_{ct} = F_{ct}; \quad S_{lf} \# F_{ld} = F_{ld};$$

$$B_{vr} \# F_{ct} = F_{ld}; \quad B_{vr} \# F_{ld} = F_{ct}; \quad F_{ct} \# F_{ld} = B_{vr};$$

$$S_{lf} \# S_{lf} = S_{lf}; \quad B_{vr} \# B_{vr} = S_{lf}; \quad F_{ct} \# F_{ct} = S_{lf}; \quad \text{and}$$

$$F_{ld} \# F_{ld} = S_{lf}.$$

The first three formulas indicate that the construct Self (symbol S_{lf}) functions within Level III as an identity or neutral element in its interactions with the other three Level III constructs. The last four of the formulas indicate the self-inverse property at this level of generality. Heuristically, the fourth, fifth and sixth formulas are of most interest. In addition, they also witness to the groupness of the constructs at Level III.

135

4. Level IV Symbolic Formulas

At Level IV the number of symbolic formulas increases significantly. The total number of formulas that it is possible to write goes up to thirty-six. Thus, it is possible to write the following symbolic formulas.

a. There are seven formulas that indicate that the construct O_{rg} functions at Level IV as an identity or neutral element for the set of constructs found at that Level. For example, one can write:

$$O_{rg} \# P_{rp} = P_{rp}; \; O_{rg} \# A_{ct} = A_{ct}; \; O_{rg} \# P_{st} = P_{st};$$

$$O_{rg} \# K_{nw} = K_{nw}; \; O_{rg} \# E_{xp} = E_{xp}; \; O_{rg} \# S_{ty} = S_{ty}; \; \text{and}$$

$$O_{rg} \# V_{al} = V_{al}.$$

b. One can also write twenty-one symbolic formulas that appear to have some heuristic value. For example, one can construct sets of formulas that define each of the Level IV constructs in terms of differing interactions among the other Level IV constructs. For example, one can write:

$$P_{rp} \# A_{ct} = P_{st}; \; P_{rp} \# P_{st} = A_{ct}; \; P_{rp} \# K_{nw} = E_{xp};$$

$$P_{rp} \# E_{xp} = K_{nw}; \; P_{rp} \# S_{ty} = V_{al}; \; P_{rp} \# V_{al} = S_{ty};$$

$$A_{ct} \# P_{st} = P_{rp}; \; A_{ct} \# K_{nw} = S_{ty}; \; A_{ct} \# E_{xp} = V_{al};$$

$$A_{ct} \# S_{ty} = K_{nw}; \; A_{ct} \# V_{al} = E_{xp}; \; P_{st} \# K_{nw} = V_{al};$$

$$P_{st} \# E_{xp} = S_{ty}; \; P_{st} \# S_{ty} = E_{xp}; \; P_{st} \# V_{al} = K_{nw};$$

$$K_{nw} \# E_{xp} = P_{rp}; \; K_{nw} \# S_{ty} = A_{ct}; \; K_{nw} \# V_{al} = P_{st};$$

$$E_{xp} \# S_{ty} = P_{st}; \; E_{xp} \# V_{al} = A_{ct}; \; \text{and } S_{ty} \# V_{al} = P_{rp}.$$

Some of these twenty-one formulas at Level IV have more sheer heuristic potential than others. Two examples may illustrate this point.

<u>First</u>, consider the Level IV construct of Knowledge (symbol K_{nw}). Three of the twenty-one formulas conclude with this construct: i.e.,

$$P_{rp} \# E_{xp} = K_{nw}; \; A_{ct} \# S_{ty} = K_{nw}; \; \text{and } P_{st} \# V_{al} = K_{nw}.$$

These three formulas indicate that the construct Knowledge (K_{nw}), as a contributory or constituting construct

136

of Personality (P_{ty}), is the result of three specific interactions: (1) Purpose and Experience; (2) Activity and Society; and (3) Persistence and Values. Therefore, to understand the construct Knowledge as part of Personality, one must be concerned with three dynamics that could be termed purposive experience, societal activity, and value persistence. This trio of formulas suggests to us that the group structure model points one into dynamics that are not always associated with the construct Knowledge, although reflection may well lead one to conclude that the kinds of Knowledge suggested by these dynamics very probably are operative in the formation of human personality. Minimally, this trio provides model-based hypotheses.

Second, consider the Level IV construct Purpose (symbol P_{rp}). Again, three of the twenty-one formulas conclude with this construct: i.e.,

$$A_{ct} \# P_{st} = P_{rp}; \quad K_{nw} \# E_{xp} = P_{rp}; \quad \text{and } S_{ty} \# V_{al} = P_{rp}.$$

These three formulas indicate that the construct Purpose (P_{rp}), as a constituting or contributory construct of Personality (P_{ty}), is the result of three specific interactions: (1) Activity and Persistence; (2) Knowledge and Experience; and (3) Society and Values. Therefore, to understand the construct Purpose as part of Personality, one must be concerned with three dynamics that could be termed persistent activity, experiential knowledge, and societal values. This trio of dynamics suggests that it is useful to distinguish between each dynamic, and to recognize that individual activity (persistent activity), personal history (experiential knowledge), and social context (societal values) converge to form Purpose in Personality. Thus, study of what can be called purposiveness in humans involves considering, at this level of generality and within this model, these three dynamics. Again, minimally, one has three model-based hypotheses.

c. At Level IV there are eight other formulas that can be written. However, all eight formulas illustrate the self-inverse property of each of the constructs. Thus, one could write a formula that indicated that each Level IV construct interacts with itself and results in the identity or neutral element for Level IV. Since the first seven formulas illustrated how the construct Organism (symbol O_{rg}) functioned as an identity element, one could write a string of equivalences, like the following:

137

$$O_{rg} \mathbin{\#} O_{rg} = P_{rp} \mathbin{\#} P_{rp} = A_{ct} \mathbin{\#} A_{ct} = P_{st} \mathbin{\#} P_{st} = K_{nw} \mathbin{\#}$$

$$K_{nw} = E_{xp} \mathbin{\#} E_{xp} = S_{ty} \mathbin{\#} S_{ty} = V_{al} \mathbin{\#} V_{al} = O_{rg}.$$

With this string of eight equivalences, the full set of
thirty-six formulas for Level IV inter-construct interactions has been displayed.

5. Constituting and Inter-Level Formulas

Somewhat earlier the symbol + was proposed for the relation
of constituting, as applied to inter-Level relationship in
the group structure model. Using this symbol, it is possible to write symbolic formulas that express the hierarchical
nature of the group structure. However, rather than explain
them in words, the following symbolic formulas affirm that
Personality (symbol P_{ty}) is constituted by interrelations
of sets of varying numbers of constructs at different levels
of generality in the group structure model. The formulas in
Figure 6.3 may have not only symbolic elegance but heuristic
value, for they suggest that it is possible that a good deal
of "talk" about human personality involves mixed or multi-
Level statements. For example, the point seems relatively
unchallengeable to affirm that human personality involves
the Self, Behavior and Environment. If reduced to the sym-
bolization of Figures 6.2 and 6.3, such an affirmation would
be written as:

$$P_{ty} = ((S_{lf} + B_{vr}) + E_{vr})$$

The parenthesization indicates the difference in Level of
the three constructs: the constructs S_{lf} and B_{vr} are Level
III constructs, while the construct E_{vr} is a Level II construct. Actually, according to the group structure model,
this affirmation is equivalent to affirming that Personality
is the result of a Person-Environment interaction, since

$$P_{sn} = (S_{lf} + B_{vr}).$$

We suspect that part of the difficulty encountered in using
such a three-part analysis of Personality is a function of
the mixed, multi-level nature of the affirmation. Therefore, while such multi-level affirmations are both possible
and symbolizable, we wonder if they may not prove to be
more of a hindrance to the unwary than a help to the
cautious.

6. The Algebra of the Hierarchy

In Table 4.4 an abstract group of Order 16 isomorphic with
the maximum inherent order of the original group of elements

$$P_{ty} =$$

P_{ty}			Level I
$= ($	P_{sn}	$+$	E_{vr}	$)$	Level II

$$P_{ty} = P_{ty} \qquad \text{Level I}$$

$$= (\ P_{sn}\ +\ E_{vr}\ ) \qquad \text{Level II}$$

$$= ((\ S_{lf}\ +\ B_{vr}\ )+(\ F_{ct}\ +\ F_{ld}\ )) \qquad \text{Level III}$$

$$= (((O_{rg} + P_{rp})+(\ A_{ct} + P_{st}\ ))+((\ K_{nw} + E_{xp})+(\ S_{ty} + V_{al}\ ))) \qquad \text{Level IV}$$

$$= ((((U+E)+(S+V))+((A+G)+(C+J)))+(((D+L)+(H+R))+((M+W)+(X+P)))) \qquad \text{Level V}$$

Figure 6.3. Symbolic formulas for personality at differing levels.

139

was displayed. In that figure, the abstract group was
formed using the inter-element operation of algebraic multiplication. Since operations of both multiplication and addition are amenable to the commutative property, we wondered
about the likelihood that one could construct the hierarchical structure of levels of generality upon the base of the
abstract group in Table 4.4. The operation of constituting
seemed somewhat analogous to algebraic or logical addition.
When we tried, we found that a hierarchical group structure
became evident. As we considered the results of using algebraic addition with pairs of Level V elements of the abstract group from Table 4.4, we came to some interesting
conclusions.

First, the reduced result for Level IV indicated a common
term (i.e., (1+a)), plus a series of multipliers (i.e., I,
b, c, bc, d, bd, cd and bcd) that, in themselves, constituted an Abelian group formed from an identity element and
three generators (i.e., b, c, and d).

Second, as the algebraic addition was carried forward to the
next higher level, Level III, the reduced result indicated a
complex common term composed of two parenthesized expressions (i.e., ((1+b)(1+a))), plus a series of multipliers
(i.e., I, c, d and cd) that, in themselves, constituted an
Abelian group formed from an identity element and two generators (i.e., c and d).

Third, at the next higher level of generality at Level II a
similar phenomenon was encountered: there was a complex
common term composed of three parenthesized expressions
(i.e., ((1+c)(1+b)(1+a))), plus two multipliers (i.e., I and
d) that constituted an Abelian group formed from an identity
element and one generator (i.e., d). This Level II group is
of Order 2, and involves the self-inverse property of the
multiplier elements (i.e., $d^2 = I = I^2$).

Fourth, when the algebraic addition was carried out to its
final conclusion, the result was a single multiplier (i.e.,
I, the identity element) and a complex common term that consisted of four parenthesized terms (i.e., ((1+d)(1+c)(1+b)
(1+a))) to make an Abelian group of Order 1.

The appearance of successively larger and more complex
common terms as the hierarchy of levels of generality was created suggests to us that, as one uses more and more general
terms, the number of necessary, albeit usually unstated, assumptions grows. If the common terms are taken as analogs of
such assumptions, their presence represents in abstract form a
clear implication of the hierarchical structure. In fact,
these results suggest that the hierarchical order, pattern, and

regularity so far discerned in the parent group of Order 16 are truly inherent in the <u>structure</u> of this particular Abelian group. Thus, the group structure <u>qua</u> model is independent of the specific elements originally posited, which is to say that it is a model of considerable power and generality.

Although we will not demonstrate the fact, we will point out that if any of the complex terms for any of the constructs at Level IV, III, II or I were to be multiplied out, the results will be the recreation of only those Level V elements that are involved in a hierarchical relation with that particular construct. Thus, one can supply an abstract mathematical demonstration of a structure isomorphic to the previously discerned hierarchically arranged series of levels of generality, which is a structure isomorphic to the maximum inherent order found in the original group of Order 16 with which we began.

The fact that algebraic addition was the operation used to model the operation of "constituting" an abstract hierarchical structure of levels of generality, while algebraic multiplication was the operation used to model the operation of "interaction" involved in creating a table of interaction results for this abstract group, should not be overlooked. We think these conditions strongly suggest that the operations of "interaction" and "constituting" are theoretically and actually different. We suspect that this conclusion means that neither personality <u>per se</u> nor a theory of personality can function adequately with a simple dependence upon a single interconstruct operation. For example, a Personality theory needs two different operations to accommodate both <u>intra</u>-level interconstruct interaction and the <u>inter</u>-level processes of differentiation and de-differentiation. Within the limits of this group structure, we see reason to affirm a complexity without giving up the task of modeling that complexity, which we call human personality.

IDENTIFYING IMPLICATIONS OF THE MODEL

The hierarchical structure of levels of generality has been explored and, finally, identified with an abstract mathematical process. Certain implications of a heuristic value also have been identified along the way. In Figure 6.4 the results of this process have been combined symbolically into a composite paradigm.

In Figure 6.4 the paradigm of a hierarchical structure is displayed and, at each of the first four levels of generality, four entries per construct are recorded. First, the construct title proposed in Figure 6.1 is listed. Second, the reduced abstract notion is recorded immediately below the construct's

CONSTRUCTS

I (1+d)(1+c)(1+b)(1+a)   PERSONALITY (P_{ty})

PERSON	ENVIRONMENT
$(1''')$ I (1+c)(1+b)(1+a) (P_{sn})	(a''') d (1+c)(1+b)(1+a) (E_{vr})

SELF	BEHAVIOR	FUNCTION	FIELD
$(1'')$ I (1+b)$\{$(1+a)$\}$ (S_{lf})	(a'') c (1+b)$\{$(1+a)$\}$ (B_{vr})	(b'') d (1+b)$\{$(1+a)$\}$ (F_{ct})	(c'') cd (1+b)$\{$(1+a)$\}$ (F_{ld})

ORGANISM	PURPOSE	ACTIVITY	PERSISTENCE	KNOWLEDGE	EXPERIENCE	SOCIETY	VALUES
$\frac{I}{1}(1+a)$ $(1')(O_{rg})$	$\frac{b}{a}(1+a)$ $(a')(P_{rp})$	$\frac{c}{b}(1+a)$ $(b')(A_{ct})$	$\frac{bc}{c}(1+a)$ $(c')(P_{st})$	$\frac{d}{d}(1+a)$ $(d')(K_{nw})$	$\frac{bd}{e}(1+a)$ $(e')(E_{xp})$	$\frac{cd}{f}(1+a)$ $(f')(S_{ty})$	$\frac{bcd}{g}(1+a)$ $(g')(V_{al})$
$\frac{U}{1}\,\frac{a}{}$ $\frac{H}{a}\,\frac{a}{}$	$\frac{S}{b}\,\frac{b}{}$ $\frac{V}{ab}\,\frac{o}{}$	$\frac{A}{o}\,\frac{d}{}$ $\frac{G}{ac}\,\frac{e}{}$	$\frac{C}{bc}\,\frac{f}{}$ $\frac{J}{abc}\,\frac{g}{}$	$\frac{D}{d}\,\frac{h}{}$ $\frac{L}{ad}\,\frac{i}{}$	$\frac{H}{bd}\,\frac{j}{}$ $\frac{R}{abd}\,\frac{k}{}$	$\frac{M}{cd}\,\frac{l}{}$ $\frac{W}{acd}\,\frac{m}{}$	$\frac{X}{bcd}\,\frac{n}{}$ $\frac{P}{abcd}\,\frac{o}{}$

The Uniqueness Set of Four "Elements"	The Motivational Set of Four "Elements"	The Short-term Set of Four "Elements"	The Long-term Set of Four "Elements"

Figure 6.4. Composite paradigm of a hierarchical structure.

title. Third, the general mathematical symbol for the construct within the level of generality from Tables 4.1 and Figure 5.1 is recorded within parentheses below and to the left of
the abstract notation. Fourth, the construct symbol from Figure 6.2 is listed and enclosed by parentheses below and to the
right of the abstract notation. These four entries in the
cells in Figure 6.4 are all equivalences.

The common term associated with each of the constructs in
Levels I, II, III and IV tends to become more and more complex
(albeit in an ordered manner) as one moves conceptually up from
Level V toward Level I. If our suggestion to interpret these
common terms as indicators of unstated assumptions involved at
each higher level of generality is followed, the abstract group
structure model suggests some interesting ideas. Specifically,
that model seems to suggest the following four potentially
heuristic conclusions.

1. At Level IV a common assumption of all constructs is a pervasive influence of the first generator element (i.e., element a, or E (Endowments)). Thus, to converse in terms of
   the constructs Organism, Purpose, Activity, Persistence,
   Knowledge, Experience, Society and Values involves a necessary assumption of the pervasive influence of Endowments.
   The model suggests that the construct Endowments does not
   "disappear," in the sense that it ceases to be influential,
   although it does disappear from the specific set of eight
   constructs used at this level of generality. Instead, Endowments is both subsumed by the Level IV construct Organism
   and, symbolically, becomes a Level-pervasive assumption
   through the common terms. This is a disappearing act with a
   difference: Endowments drops out of the set of language
   symbols or construct titles, at Level IV, but is still
   operative in a truly pervasive manner.

2. At Level III a common assumption of all constructs is a pervasive influence of the first and second generator elements
   (i.e., elements a and b, or E (Endowments) and S (Self-
   Image)). Thus, to converse in terms of the constructs Self,
   Behavior, Function, and Field involves a necessary but complex assumption about the pervasive influence of both Endowments and Self-Image. Once again, the Level III constructs
   involve Level V elements as unstated assumptions. Although
   both elements "disappear," they remain (through the necessary albeit tacit assumptions) operative and pervasively influential. Conversation at this level of generality, according to the group structure model, involves a tacit recognition of the influence of other less general constructs
   upon all of the constructs within this particular level of
   generality.

143

3. At Level II a common assumption of both constructs at this level is a pervasive influence of the first, second, and third generator elements (i.e., elements a, b and c, or E (Endowments), S (Self-Image) and A (Action)). Thus, to converse about the two constructs Person and Environment and their interaction in the constituting of Personality involves the necessary and even more complex assumption that Endowments, Self-Image, and Action are pervasively influential upon both the construct Person and the construct Environment. Once again, the "disappearance" is a matter of the level of generality of the constructs: the operative force is not denied, although it is shifted to a tacit acknowledgment.

4. At Level I the process finds a kind of culmination. At this level the model indicates that there must be an assumption of a pervasive influence of all four generator elements (i.e., elements a, b, c, and d, or E (Endowments), S (Self-Image), A (Action), and D (Decision Making)). The abstract notation for Level I suggests that conversation about Personality per se, conversation at a totally holistic level of generality, inescapably involves a large and complex assumption about the pervasive, complex influence of Endowments, Self-Image, Action, and Decision Making in a dynamic, multiplicative interaction with one another.

Observations

We note that the generator elements become involved as assumptions in complex terms in the order they originally were added to the group to create Table 4.4. That is, element a is the first of the generator elements, while elements b, c, and d are the second, third, and fourth generators, respectively. As a result, one could interpret Figure 6.4 as suggesting that the element standing in the multiplier position in relation to a complex common term represented (at that level of generality) a certain entry-point to understanding the specific construct. If one were to take this suggestion seriously, then some or all of the following eight observations may prove to be heuristic:

1. Element I as a Multiplier.

   Element I, or that "uniqueness" which has been posited as an identity or neutral element for the group, may be an entry-point for understanding the constructs Personality (Level I), Person (Level II), Self (Level III), and Organism (Level IV). This idea appears to be a model-generated suggestion that these four constructs require one to have a radical concern for the individual in all his or her particularity, difference or "uniqueness."

2. Element d as a Multiplier.

Element d, the Level V element Decision Making, may be an entry-point for understanding the constructs Knowledge (Level IV), Function (Level III), and Environment (Level II). This idea also appears to be a model-generated suggestion that choice (the prototypical aspect of Decision Making) is the conceptual entry-point to understanding the constructs Knowledge, Function, and Environment. This idea dictates a radical insistence upon the importance of individual choice for understanding contributions of any of these constructs to a human personality. This idea also seems similar to Piaget's observation that the individual contributes as much to his interaction with his environment (i.e., his socialization) as the environment contributes to him by way of an outside force (i.e., as a socializing force) (Piaget & Inhelder, 1969).

3. Element b as a Multiplier.

Element b, the Level V element Self-Image, may be an entry-point for understanding the construct Purpose (Level IV). This idea can be interpreted as a model-generated suggestion that what can be identified as Purpose is, at least initially, best understood in terms of Self-Image. This seems like a relatively reasonable idea, although it puts strong emphasis upon the importance of self-image when considering an individual's purposiveness or lack of purpose. We suspect that this also could be used to argue for a particular approach to either diagnosis or prescription in education, counseling, or clinical practice.

4. Element c as a Multiplier.

Element c, the Level V element Action, may be an entry-point for understanding the constructs Activity (Level IV) and Behavior (Level III). This model-generated idea suggests that one begins to understand Activity and Behavior through focusing upon the overt and the observable. While this idea seems quite unexceptionable (e.g., it is almost a matter of definitions), it is an almost radical suggestion to focus attention upon the overt and observable when considering the part played by the constructs Activity and Behavior in creation of a Personality.

5. The Element bc as a Multiplier.

The element bc, the Level V element Courage, may be an entry-point for understanding the construct Persistence (Level IV). This model-generated suggestion seems relatively reasonable, although it is worth emphasizing that the group structure model does generate the suggestion.

6. Element bd as a Multiplier.

Element bd, the Level V element entitled Home Resources, may be an entry-point for understanding the Level IV construct Experience. This model-generated idea could be interpreted as suggesting that the contribution of Experience to Personality is best understood by first trying to understand the individual's sense of the range of resources available to him or her in the "home." Since definition of this Level V element suggested that, conceptually, it was like a ratio between objective facts and subjective perceptions, this suggestion emphasizes strongly the importance of understanding an individual's home setting (especially in terms of "resources" available to members of that "home" setting). This idea seems somewhat similar to a host of suggestions that are, we believe, basic to several schools of clinical practice.

7. The Element cd as a Multiplier.

Element cd, the Level V element entitled Measures of Character, may be an entry-point to understanding the constructs Society (Level IV) and Field (Level III). This model-generated idea suggests that the constructs Society and Field, as contributors to Personality, are best understood initially through understanding how an individual perceives his or her "place" within the world as known. As far as either Personality or a theory of Personality is concerned, this idea could be interpreted as a radical plea to understand abstractions such as Society or Field through the eyes of the participating individual. Perhaps, unlike sociological or political understandings, such general constructs may influence Personality initially in terms of an individual's known world and his or her sense of place within that world. (As the reader may recall, this idea of "place" was stressed in the definition for element M, or cd, in Chapter 4.) Thus, the model seems to have generated a radically individual centered entry-point, which might serve as a caution that, for a human Personality, larger societal abstractions tend to become reduced to a matter of an individual's "place" within what may be recognized and labeled as the locus of one's existence. This suggestion seems to us to be similar to an idea that is common to much anthropological field study.

8. Element bcd as a Multiplier.

Element bcd, the Level V element Evaluation, may be an
entry-point for understanding the construct Values (Level
IV). This idea could be interpreted as a model-generated
suggestion that, at least as far as Personality construction
is concerned, the construct Values can best be understood by
focusing attention upon the set of available (and used)
skills for comparing actuality to standards. This idea
seems to be a rather radical plea to approach study of "values" (at least as a part of the study of Personality)
through an individual's ability to evaluate (i.e., to compare and contrast what is with what known and accepted
standards say should be). Without denying a reality to values per se, this idea seems to be an operationalization of
values as contributors to human personality. The radicalism
of this model-generated idea may be that it appears to offer
a pathway to understanding what an individual's "values" are
through assessment of performance in specific or manageable
tasks.

These eight implications of the group structure model as
the model generates a hierarchically arranged series of levels
of constructs may be enough to suggest why we conclude that
this model has considerable heuristic value. In a sense, each
of these suggestions or ideas is isomorphic with common experience. If that is so, it would affirm a form of validity for
this model. In the following chapters we wish to look at some
other reasons for advancing the group structure model, as well
as to identify some interesting hypotheses that further consideration of that model has generated.

7

EXTENSIONS WITH IMPLICATIONS

Friendship is a persistent human phenomenon. Admittedly, it is not a particularly precise concept, but it is a phenomenon admitting of degrees. For example, imagine a <u>Querier</u> (Q) and a <u>Responder</u> (R) talking about three people, and notice the difference in the answers that are given to queries about these three "friends" of the responder.

Q1: How well do you know Alice Brown?

R1: Oh, I recognize who she is. I think I once had a class with her.

Doesn't she live off campus?

Q2: Is Alice Brown a friend of yours?

R2: Well, yes. Actually, more of an acquaintance.

Q3: All right. How well do you know Carol Dowling?

R3: Fairly well. I see her pretty frequently; in classes and at the Student Center, you know. Yeah, she's a great gal! She really can dig into a project when she wants to: we worked on a committee together last semester, you know. I think I know Carol fairly well.

Q4: Good. Is Carol Dowling a friend of yours?

R4: Sure. Yeah, I guess you'd say she and I are fairly good friends. We work together pretty well, of course.

Q5: Fine. Now, how well do you know Ellen Farley?

R₅: Really quite well. Ellen is actually one of my best
    friends. She and I study together often. She likes
    Mozart on the record player when we study. Her father is
    a doctor, you know, and she has five brothers. Of course,
    she really likes only two of them! But she's a great per-
    son to be with: she's attentive; a real listener. Yet,
    when she has something to say, she does so in no uncer-
    tain terms. Yeah, I know Ellen well.

Q₆: All right. Is Ellen Farley a friend of yours?

R₆: Sure. I guess you'd say that we're the best of friends.

In this imaginative conversation the Responder identifies
one acquaintance and two friends. However, these three persons
can be ranged along a continuum defined by the amount of information about each person available to the Responder. Obviously
the Responder has least information about Alice Brown (the acquaintance). Equally obvious, the Responder has somewhat more
information about Carol Dowling (the fairly good friend) and,
actually, a good deal of information about Ellen Farley (the
best friend). In this conversation, "depth," "extent" or "degree" of friendship matches depth, extent, or degree of information available to the Responder.

This conversation illustrates just one point: in normal
friendships a correlation exists between "degree" of friendship
and "amount" or "detail" of information available to a friend.
This correlation between degree of friendship and specificity
of available information seems to be a normal human phenomenon.
However, the normality of this phenomenon raises an interesting
question vis-a-vis the group structure model. Is there any
such phenomenon modeled by the group structure? If so, the
model would gain strength, for it would "model" yet another
aspect of personality: personality as seen through eyes of
one's friends.

EXTENDING THE MODEL TOWARD INCREASING SPECIFICITY

In the following pages we engage in a rather theoretical
extension of the group structure model. We do so for two reasons: first, because the extended group structure seems to offer a model-generated analog to the phenomenon of friendship,
particularly the increasingly specific knowledge about what
makes a friend particularly himself or herself or unique; and
second, because extension of the group structure suggests that
the hierarchy of levels of generality is conceptually unfinished and extendable. As Piaget noted, each element in a
structure is both form to that which it subsumes and content

to some higher form which subsumes it (Piaget, 1971). Also, an extendable hierarchy of levels of generality seems related to Platt's observations about the value of both an immediately supra-ordinate level and an immediately sub-ordinate level in any hierarchically arranged system of concepts. Platt's point was that both the supra-ordinate and the sub-ordinate levels were needed if growth from level to level was either to be accomplished or understood (Platt, 1970).

In Figure 7.1 the same procedure that was used to generate Abelian groups of Orders 2, 4, 8 and 16 has been used to generate theoretical Abelian groups of Orders 32, 64 and 128. The relationship between the groups of Order 16 and Order 32 is, for example, the same as that between the groups of Order 8 and Order 16. That is, between levels in the group structure model there are both hereditary and hierarchical relationships.

The theoretical construction of an Abelian group of Order 32 therefore allows one to identify a series of symbols that can represent a sub-ordinate level of elements which, in pairs, constitutes each of the 16 Level V elements. As we suggested in Chapter 6, this inter-level relationship of constituting is similar to algebraic addition. Thus, the new Level VI group of 32 elements identifies what, through a process of minimum differentiation, one would expect to encounter as one became more and more specific about the meaning of the 16 Level V elements.

In Figure 7.1 the basic procedure involved creating an Abelian group from the Cartesian product of a series of cyclic groups of Order 2 that had generating elements a, b, c, d, e, etc. This procedure was originally identified from Fox's work (Fox, 1970). However, it is important to notice two things about this procedure: (1) the Abelian groups generated in this way relate to one another in a generally hereditary manner, and (2) the meaning of the abstract mathematical symbols (e.g., the a, b, c, and d) is determined strictly through intra-level relationships until, and unless, all higher levels have been derived from a baseline lowest level. An example of such a derivation of successively higher levels from a lowest baseline level was displayed in Figure 6.4. An hereditary inter-level relationship means that a pair of ordinate-level elements constitutes, via a process of minimal de-differentiation similar to algebraic addition, a next-higher supra-ordinate-level construct. That the abstract mathematical symbols for the generating elements are intra-level determined in their meaning seems to be implicit in such an hereditary inter-level relationship. This idea also forces one to focus attention upon the function of generating, without presuming that a generator element a at Level IV, for instance, is necessarily the same as the generator element a at Level V.

Level V (Order 16)	Level VI (Order 32)	Level VII (Order 64)	Level VIII (Order 128)

UNIQUENESS

```
                                          ⎧ I  ───────  ⎧ I
                          ⎧ I  ─────────  ⎨             ⎨ a*
                          ⎪              ⎩ a*           ⎪ b*
U ─────── I  ─────────    ⎨                             ⎩ ab
                          ⎪              ⎧ b* ───────  ⎧ c*
                          ⎩ a* ────────  ⎨             ⎨ ac
                                         ⎩ ab           ⎪ bc
                                                        ⎩ abc
```

ENDOWMENTS

```
                                          ⎧ c* ───────  ⎧ d*
                          ⎧ b* ─────────  ⎨             ⎨ ad
                          ⎪              ⎩ ac            ⎪ bd
E ─────── a*  ─────────   ⎨                             ⎩ abd
                          ⎪              ⎧ bc ───────  ⎧ cd
                          ⎩ ab ────────  ⎨             ⎨ acd
                                         ⎩ abc          ⎪ bcd
                                                        ⎩ abcd
```

SELF-IMAGE

```
                                          ⎧ d* ───────  ⎧ e*
                          ⎧ c* ─────────  ⎨             ⎨ ae
                          ⎪              ⎩ ad            ⎪ be
S ─────── b*  ─────────   ⎨                             ⎩ abe
                          ⎪              ⎧ bd ───────  ⎧ ce
                          ⎩ ac ────────  ⎨             ⎨ ace
                                         ⎩ abd          ⎪ bce
                                                        ⎩ abce
```

VISION

```
                                          ⎧ cd ───────  ⎧ de
                          ⎧ bc ─────────  ⎨             ⎨ ade
                          ⎪              ⎩ acd           ⎪ bde
V ─────── ab  ─────────   ⎨                             ⎩ abde
                          ⎪              ⎧ bcd ──────  ⎧ cde
                          ⎩ abc ───────  ⎨             ⎨ acde
                                         ⎩ abcd         ⎪ bcde
                                                        ⎩ abcde
```

Figure 7.1. A theoretical exploration of Levels V, VI, VII, and VIII. Part A-- First four elements of a parent group of Order 16.

152

Level V (Order 16)	Level VI (Order 32)	Level VII (Order 64)	Level VIII (Order 128)

ACTION

A ——— c*
- d*
  - e* ——— f*, af
  - ae ——— bd, abf
- ad
  - be ——— cf, acf
  - abe ——— bcf, abcf

GROWTH

G ——— ac
- bd
  - ce ——— df, adf
  - ace ——— bdf, abdf
- abd
  - bce ——— cdf, acdf
  - abce ——— bcdf, abcdf

COURAGE

C ——— bc
- cd
  - de ——— ef, aef
  - ade ——— bef, abef
- acd
  - bde ——— cef, acef
  - abde ——— bcef, abcef

JUDGMENT

J ——— abc
- bcd
  - cde ——— def, adef
  - acde ——— bdef, abdef
- abcd
  - bcde ——— cdef, acdef
  - abcde ——— bcdef, abcdef

Figure 7.1. A theoretical exploration of Levels V, VI, VII, and VIII. Part B--Second four elements of a parent group of Order 16.

153

Level V (Order 16)	Level VI (Order 32)	Level VII (Order 64)	Level VIII (Order 128)

DECISION MAKING

D ———— d* ————
- e* ————
  - f* ————
    - g*
    - ag
    - bg
    - abg
  - af ————
    - cg
    - acg
    - bcg
    - abcg
- ae ————
  - bf ————
  - abf ————

LEARNING

L ———— ad ————
- be ————
  - cf ————
    - dg
    - adg
    - bdg
    - abdg
  - acf ————
    - cdg
    - acdg
    - bcdg
    - abcdg
- abe ————
  - bcf ————
  - abcf ————

HOME RESOURCES

H ———— bd ————
- ce ————
  - df ————
    - eg
    - aeg
    - beg
    - abeg
  - adf ————
    - ceg
    - aceg
    - bceg
    - abceg
- ace ————
  - bdf ————
  - abdf ————

ROLES

R ———— abd ————
- bce ————
  - cdf ————
    - deg
    - adeg
    - bdeg
    - abdeg
  - acdf ————
    - cdeg
    - acdeg
    - bcdeg
    - abcdeg
- abce ————
  - bcdf ————
  - abcdf ————

Figure 7.1. A theoretical exploration of Levels V, VI, VII, and VIII. Part C--Third four elements of a parent group of Order 16.

154

Level V (Order 16)	Level VI (Order 32)	Level VII (Order 64)	Level VIII (Order 128)

MEASURES OF CHARACTER

M ————— cd —————
- de —————
  - ef —————
    - fg
    - afg
  - aef —————
    - bfg
    - abfg
- ade —————
  - bef —————
    - cfg
    - acfg
  - abef —————
    - bcfg
    - abcfg

WORLD

W ————— acd —————
- bde —————
  - cef —————
    - dfg
    - adfg
  - acef —————
    - bdfg
    - abdfg
- abde —————
  - bcef —————
    - cdfg
    - acdfg
  - abcef —————
    - bcdfg
    - abcdfg

EVALUATION

X ————— bcd —————
- cde —————
  - def —————
    - efg
    - aefg
  - adef —————
    - befg
    - abefg
- acde —————
  - bdef —————
    - cefg
    - acefg
  - abdef —————
    - bcefg
    - abcefg

PHILOSOPHY

P ————— abcd —————
- bcde —————
  - cdef —————
    - defg
    - adefg
  - acdef —————
    - bdefg
    - abdefg
- abcde —————
  - bcdef —————
    - cdefg
    - acdefg
  - abcdef —————
    - bcdefg
    - abcdefg

Figure 7.1. A theoretical exploration of Levels V, VI, VII and VIII. Part D--Fourth four elements of a parent group of Order 16.

Our point is simply that an a is a general mathematical
symbol for the _first_ generating element in any level of generality, just as an I is a general mathematical symbol for the
identity or neutral element at any level of generality. Specifically, this means that the symbol I successively represents
the group structure elements Person (Level II), Self (Level
III), Organism (Level IV), and Uniqueness (Level V). In the
same way, the first generating element (i.e., the element symbolized as a) successively represents the group structure elements Environment (Level II), Behavior (Level III), Purpose
(Level IV), and Endowments (Level V).

Although the reader may have sensed that some such convention was operative, our experience indicates that it is useful
to stress this point. The hierarchy of levels of generality
appears to be consistently hereditary, although the inter-level
relation of constituting is different than the intra-level relation of interaction. These two relations must be kept separate and distinct. If they are, when Figure 7.1 displays a
series of a elements at Levels V, VI, VII, and VIII, the reader
will recognize that the only thing common to those elements
across all four levels is that, within the level, each a element functions as the first generator element for that level's
Abelian group. The actual, specific meaning to be assigned to
each of these a elements is different.

For example, at Level V the symbol a represents the element
ment titled Endowments. However, at Level VI the symbol a rer-
resents an untitled element that is a pair-partner with the
Level VI element symbolized as I in the constituting of Level
V's element I, Uniqueness. The element a is not the same at
Levels V and VI. This process continues as one moves downward
from Level V through Levels VI, VII, and VIII. The process
represents what we have earlier termed minimal differentiation,
one of the two complementary inter-level processes.

We believe that this excursus into what may have been a
stressing of the obvious is justified, because inter-level relationships are an important aspect of the group structure
model that should be understood as precisely as possible.
Moreover, the process outlined in Figure 7.1 suggests that the
group structure, as it is extended downward from Level V, exhibits a phenomenon that seems analogous to the phenomenon of
human friendship.

As one moves down from Level V to Levels VI, VII, and VIII
one encounters levels of generality that (theoretically) are
increasingly specific. As one becomes more and more specific
however an increasing number of the generating elements for
these more specific level groups tends to become subsumed under
the Level V element I, or Uniqueness. This process suggests to

us the phenomenon of friendship, since as the degree of friendship increases, there appears to be an increase in the amount,
range, and specificity of information about a friend that is
available to the befriender. The model suggests that what at
Level V is simply recognized as a philosophically posited
attribute—Uniqueness—becomes, with each successive increase
in level of specificity, more and more separated into recog-
nizably specific constituting elements. While the reality of a
friend's uniqueness does not disappear as the friendship develops, the uniqueness does tend to become increasingly specified
as the relationship deepens.

The phenomenon of friendship is a reasonably common experience. The group structure seems to operate so that it does,
in fact, model a basic reality of that phenomenon. With increasing friendship, for example, one becomes less and less
aware of one's friend as representative of some class of humans,
or of some type of personality, and more and more aware of the
specific particularities of the friend's personality: one be-
one becomes increasingly aware of the friend's uniqueness. Because we regard this phenomenon as widespread, pervasive, and
fundamental, we regard the ability of the group structure to
generate an analog as a sign of the power of the model. At the
very least, it seems to us to be yet another indication of the
validity of this model.

Given what we know about the way a hereditary hierarchy of
constructs may be developed, it is possible to generalize this
process into another figure that shows that an increasing number of intra-level-specific generating elements do tend to become subsumed "under" the Level V identity element, Uniqueness.
This is presented in Figure 7.2, which gives in tabular form an
indication of how the process of minimum differentiation might
be extended to create very large Abelian groups of, presumedly,
highly specific elements. However, for our present purposes
the identification and naming of constructs "below" Level V
will not be attempted. Still, it does seem useful to recognize
that the Level V elements represent both a "lower" level of
relative specificity (e.g., vis-a-vis Levels I through IV) and
a "higher" level of generality (e.g., vis-a-vis the theoretically identifiable Levels from VI "downward").

Once again, the group structure model seems to be inherently hierarchical. It can be regarded as created by either of
two complementary processes: minimum differentiation or minimum de-differentation. At each of the identifiable levels in
Figure 7.2 the level-specific constructs function as an intra-
level Abelian group that contains a number of elements equal to
two raised to a power that is one less than the number of the
Level. For example, a Level V group has $2^{(5-1)}$, or 16

Level Number	Number of Elements in the Group	Number of Generating Elements Per Level V Generator					Proportion Elements	
		UNIQUENESS I	ENDOWMENTS a	SELF-IMAGE b	ACTION c	DECISION MAKING d	Subsumed By U	Subsumed By E, S, A and D
V	16	0	1 a	1 b	1 c	1 d	0.0000	1.0000
VI	32	1 a	1 b	1 c	1 d	1 e	0.2000	0.8000
VII	64	2 a,b	1 c	1 d	1 e	1 f	0.3333	0.6666
VIII	128	3 a,b,c	1 d	1 e	1 f	1 g	0.4286	0.5714
IX	256	4 a,b,c,d	1 e	1 f	1 g	1 h	0.5000	0.5000
X	512	5 a,b,c,d,e	1 f	1 g	1 h	1 i	0.5555	0.4444
XI	1024	6 a,b,c,d,e,f	1 g	1 h	1 i	1 j	0.6000	0.4000
XII	2048	7 a,b,c,d,e,f,g	1 h	1 i	1 j	1 k	0.6364	0.3636
XIII	4096	8 a,b,c,d,e,f,g,h	1 i	1 j	1 k	1 l	0.6667	0.3333
XIV	8192	9 a,b,c,d,e,f,g,h,i	1 j	1 k	1 l	1 m	0.6923	0.3077
XV	16384	10 a,b,c,d,e,f,g,h,i,j	1 k	1 l	1 m	1 n	0.7143	0.2857
XVI	32768	11 a,b,c,d,e,f,g,h,i,j,k	1 l	1 m	1 n	1 o	0.7333	0.2667
XVII	65536	12 a,b,c,d,e,f,g,h,i,j,k,l	1 m	1 n	1 o	1 p	0.7500	0.2500

Figure 7.2. The subsuming of generator elements under the Level V identity element in Levels VI-XVII.

elements, while a Level IV group has $2^{(4-1)}$, or 8 elements, and a Level VII group will have $2^{(7-1)}$, or 64 elements.

In Figure 7.2 the movement of level-specific generating elements into positions of constituting sub-ordinate elements of the Level V construct Uniqueness is evident. The fact is also evident in Figure 7.2 that each of the four Level V generating elements (i.e., element a (Endowments), element b (Self-Image), element c (Action), and element d (Decision Making)) always retain a level-specific generating element in each of the successively specified intra-level Abelian groups. Thus, if one posited that the 16 Level V elements presently represent a useful level of relative specificity, results of any further minimum differentiation would involve only successive specification of the constituting parts of the I construct Uniqueness, and successive specification of the active, interacting constituting parts of each of the four Level V generator elements.

The theoretical analysis implicit in Figure 7.2 suggests to us that, with increasing specificity, more and more of the constituting sub-ordinate constructs subsumed by Uniqueness (Level V) come to play increasingly powerful, influential roles in the intra-level Abelian groups constructable at the lower levels of generality. This phenomenon seems to us to be analogous to the widespread human experience of a growing, deepening, and strengthening friendship. The group structure model seems therefore to suggest a specific meaning to the observation that friendship is a way of "knowing" another person, especially in his or her particularity or uniqueness.

SELECTED IMPLICATIONS OF THE MODEL

The group structure model that we have presented implicitly raises a very old question: What is Man? We are well aware that every paradigm represents some answer to that question. We have already indicated our general agreement with Sanford's contention that we need more adequate paradigms of Man as a subject of research (Sanford, 1970). We also recognize that the Psalmist's question (Psalms 8:3-4) is still poignant in these days when the contrast between the frail human and the vastness of the Universe is as sharp or sharper than before humans knew as much about the expanses of Space. In addition, we recognize that some people regard human freedom and dignity as pernicious illusions (Skinner, 1971), while others suspect that such "illusions" are the bedrock of human existence (Lefcourt, 1973). Finally, we realize that there has been a continuing feud within the helping professions between those who emphasize Nurture and those who emphasize Nature, between empiricists and nativists, and we doubt that our work will resolve the issue.

Still, we feel bound to state our own conclusions if for no other reason than that we recognize that the question is implicit in our model of human personality. A hereditary, hierarchical structure such as the group model begs the question: How does it come to be? While we suspect we have an answer, we recognize that a full answer is somewhat like a full description of the process of psychogenesis. The model, as it stands, seems to us to be a model of a mature, developed human personality, one we would call integrated. We suspect that the group structure of the model is developed across time through the processes we have identified as differentiation and de-differentiation, that is, through both induction and deduction.

We also have noted that we see in the model suggestions of the process Piaget has called adaptation, which, in his view, is a generalization of a cycle composed of the more specific processes of assimilation and accommodation (Piaget, 1967). This suggestion seems to be a clear implication of our positing at Level II of the two constructs Person and Environment as the constituting elements of Personality (Level I). The very hierarchical nature of this group structure suggests that this basic Person–Environment interaction becomes, across time, differentiated into a series of increasingly more specific constructs at successively lower levels of generality. Moreover, it seems likely that what Piaget has termed the process of equilibration functions at each such level of generality (Piaget, 1967). In fact, equilibration may be what one means by a term like integration. This seems to be a particularly attractive way of thinking, especially if one posits a series of possible integrations (e.g., each, perhaps, situationally apropos), rather than a single goal-type integration, which may only be successively approximated.

The Level II interaction between the constructs Person and Environment appears to be similar to the Piagetian processes of assimilation and accommodation. That is, within a biological metaphor, one could speak of the Environment being (within the present abilities of the Person) assimilated into the Person and, as a result, of that Person being (within his or her abilities) accommodated to that Environment. In Structuralism, Piaget suggested that recognition of such mutuality of influence (which we have referred to as the intra-level relation of interaction) suggests a mechanism for successive construction of increasingly complex structure (Piaget, 1971). While Piaget has been primarily concerned with the epistemological question of how one knows, his paradigm for epistemological growth and development seems to be similar to the group structure model paradigm for growth and development of Personality.

The group structure model posits something much more complex than a simple "flowering" of genetic "seed." We recognize that our model's basic Level II division into Person and Environment could be interpreted as identifying a _genetic_ contribution to Personality (and we do not care to deny that!), _but_ the group structure is _not_ a model of inevitable, hereditarily determined growth and development. The construct Environment at Level II suggests that Personality itself is _constituted_ out of Person _and_ Environment and is equivalent to the _interaction_ of Person _and_ Environment. Thus, our model suggests that Personality inescapably involves an interaction between whatever genetics may contribute with whatever the societal/natural world combination may contribute. Such an interaction exists within the flow and flux of time. Therefore, the Person-Environment interaction posited by the group structure model would seem to be, of necessity, an on-going process of "constituting" that (we suspect) involves Time as an orthogonal dimension to the model itself.

The group structure model of the life-cycle of _homo sapiens_ seems to posit something more than sheer formation via either social or educational forces. While the construct Environment can be interpreted as a representation of such molding forces, this model affirms that Personality is "constituted" out of _both_ Person and Environment. Both constituting parts are implicitly and explicitly requisite, and (at Level II) they are in interaction with one another. In our model, then, neither part has any necessary priority. Both are necessary, and both are active.

If this model is perceived as failing to support either the idea that personality is a "flowering" of genetic "seeds" or that personality is the result of some social "sculpturing," one may ask if there is another appropriate metaphor to describe the process of personality formation pictured by the model. We think that within the fine arts there is such a metaphor in what is called improvisational drama. In such improvisations several things seem active: _first_, the actor is presumed to have control of the assigned role; _second_, the specifics of the role behavior emerge as the result of an interaction between the several actors within the dramatic situation; _third_, the drama itself is defined apart from the actors in only the broadest way by the director; _fourth_, the role that emerges in the course of the improvisation is a complex function of the actor's abilities, the situation created for him by the others with whom he is in improvisational interaction and, of course, the sheer possibilities of the "stage" or setting for the improvisation. The fact is apparent to us that the complex interaction of a dramatic improvisation is a reasonably good analogy for the complex of interactions posited of personality _per se_ by the group structure model (Piaget, 1971).

If the analogy of improvisational drama is accepted for what it is, a limited analogy and not an unlimited allegory, one can see elements of genuine power in the model and can recognize genuine dynamics in its interactions. This seems to be like a paradigm of Man as ". . . a symbol-using, self-reflective creature who acts as well as behaves" (Sanford, 1970, p. x). We see no need to deny either genetic or environmental factors, only a need to recognize that it is in the process of mutual interaction that there is the dynamic out of which Personality arises. These views of the model and of the human situation seem to us to be remarkably isomorphic. This isomorphism also suggests that human actions and possibilities can be modeled in terms of the group structure we have presented.

At a theoretical level, we believe that the position taken by Piaget about Man as a construction is amenable to modeling by the group structure we have presented. We feel that to see Man as the resultant of an interaction between Person and Environment (a resultant we have termed Personality) is implicitly to opt for a constructionist view of Man. Although such a construction must be viewed as a life-long, continuing process, the group structure model suggests that it may be understood at several levels of construct generality. Since, in this view of Man the human is seen to be as equally active as the environment in his or her own construction, one also can agree with Piaget that human growth and development are inherently lengthy processes that involve the successive adaptation of Man to the reality encountered. Across time that adaptation apparently is refined through something like a series of successive approximations or periods of equilibration.

In Piaget's epistemological paradigm, construction via cycles of assimilation and accommodation results in increasingly complex schemata, which are increasingly able to handle the interface between Person and Environment. Such schemata seem to us to be similar to the increasingly complex intra-level interactions positable as one moves downward in the group structure model toward ever more specific constructs. We suspect that, just as Piaget found complex schemata to be time-related and developmental, so there probably is a parallel time-relation for at least the awareness of the lower levels of generality posited by the group structure model. Thus, although we consider the total model to represent an integrated Personality, we also suspect that an awareness of that total model and an ability to use it for analysis and understanding of one's own experiences is almost certainly a greater possibility for mature individuals, although it may be open to some adolescents and young adults. We recognize that the group structure model represents an abstraction that involves an ability akin to thinking about one's own thinking. Therefore, we hypothesize that one must have the ability to use Piaget's formal operational thinking before this group structure model will be understandable.

Recognition that formal operational thinking may well be requisite to understanding the group structure model can serve as a twofold sign. As a cautionary sign, it is a reminder that a good portion of the early life-cycle is at a pre-formal operational level in respect to thinking: perhaps humans thinking at such levels can understand only simpler forms of the group structure model. As a sign of a capability, it suggests that, with development of formal operational thinking, a human may be able to understand the model and, so, use it to understand his or her own experiences. If that capability is possible, such a level of understanding may enable a human to become a conscious participant in the continuing construction of one's own Personality or, by choice, become involved in what we would term the progressive re-construction of one's own Personality. Active and conscious participation of humans in such a process of Personality re-construction seems to us to be a possibility that involves a truly drastic extension of the range of human freedom and responsibility.

The possibility of re-construction involves, we suspect, use of the group structure model of personality as a conceptual map for conscious choice from among alternative strategies for moving toward personally defined, more adequate personality structures. This possibility suggests that the model-as-map may provide a human with a degree of freedom that is normally impossible. This freedom to "get into the game" and to be an active participant in one's own construction is a part of the model-as-map process. Of course, this process would involve assuming responsibility for one's own personality. Tiedeman (1972) has thought and written extensively about this possibility under the heading of hierarchical restructuring. Therefore, in Section III, Chapter 8, we examine still further the possibilities we discern for the group structure model as a guide to achievement of new kinds of human freedom and new realms of personal responsibility for one's own continued growth and development.

* * * * * * * * * * * * * * * *

SECTION III

SELF

AS A KNOWING CONSTRUCTION

SOME POSSIBILITIES

* * * * * * * * * * * * * * * *

SECTION III

SELF AS A KNOWING CONSTRUCTION

SOME POSSIBILITIES

<u>An Overview</u>

Our theme has been simple: Man is a construction. In
this third and final Section we consider what it would mean to
conceive of designing a Self, a Self that is continually under
construction.

In Section I we presented <u>knowing</u> as a construction. The
Education Machine, which we designed to promote knowing, caused
us to recognize that people tend to give themselves away,
rather than to become responsible for their selves. Therefore,

we designed an Education Machine that created a relationship between the partially known and the human knower in which that knower repeatedly went through a cycle of differentiation and de-differentiation (or integration). We regard the repeated experience of such a cycle of integration-differentiation-reintegration as a necessary and sufficient experience for a human knower to gain an understanding of and confidence in this iterative process as the only way Man has available to "make more of himself."

We believe this understanding and this confidence must come to be a part of a human's very core being. As that happens, the human knower can comprehend that he or she can know only through an application of the decision-making process, even though that process itself offers no guarantee that knowing will result. Only the inquirer can know. No process, _qua_ process, can guarantee knowing!

Section II presented _personality_ as a construction, using Ernest Ligon's mathematical group as a structure. In addition, the six chapters of Section II were an example of the process of knowing which we ourselves used to comprehend Ligon's group as a _general_ model of personality organization. Our process consisted in an alternation between an appeal to the general and a testing of the specifics in terms of the general. In our view, this process exemplifies a scientific approach to determining what one holds to be true in the natural order of things.

In Section III, we take a final step in our presentation of _Man_ as a construction. That step involves uniting _knowing_ and _personality_. As we unite those two constructions, we come to the outline of what we would call a constructionist conception of the Self. This leads us to hope that a person can come to understand the Self as a knower and, as well, come to understand how that Self grows, or is constructed. We probe the meaning of such a process as we design what we term a Self Machine, an imaginary prosthetic device to help a Self know how it has been constructed, is being constructed and may become involved in construction of the Self that is yet to be. If and while that kind of knowing occurs, a human knower comes to understand that he or she can be a result of self designing, we regard that knowledge, and action taken in that knowledge the highest possible exercise of human freedom and human responsibility.

As we have done earlier, we can imagine the following Section as the record of the processes of our discovery. Therefore, we also can imagine those processes of discovery as examples of an extended interaction between the Education Machine and an Inquirer who set out, as we did, to explore the idea that the Self is an on-going construction. For us, of course, this imaginary interchange took place within and between the two of us at a far slower pace. But we think the analogy is close enough so that we trust this text will show something of how we thought and why we have written as we have.

Inquirer: (Connects his terminal to the Education Machine and proceeds to identify himself.)

Hello. This is INQUIRER.

Are we connected?

Education Machine: Welcome, Inquirer.

You are now connected to the Education Machine. It is good to have you back.

What would you like to do?

Inquirer: Well, you have helped me to conceive of both Knowing and Human Personality as constructions. Now I want to push the idea of construction a bit further.

Can you help me extend the idea of construction?

Education Machine: Possibly.

In what way do you want to extend the idea of construction?

Inquirer: I want to explore what it would mean if I were to do two things. First, if I were to conceive of the Self as continually under construction: a kind of perpetually unfinished project. Second, if I were to conceive of the possibility that such a self-under-construction could actually become its own designer.

Can you help me do these two things?

Education Machine: If I understand you correctly, I think so.

Do you want to take up those two things in the order you have listed them, or is there some other order in which you wish to consider them?

Inquirer: I am satisfied with the order in which I listed them them.

Please proceed.

Education Machine: Thank you.

Let me be certain that I understand what you intend to do. You wish to consider first what it means to conceive of the Self as a continuing construction.

Education Machine:	Then you wish to consider what it means to conceive of a Self being designed, as it were, by itself.
	If I have understood your intention, please type RIGHT.
Inquirer:	RIGHT.
	Please proceed.
Education Machine:	Let me review for you where we have been, up to this point in our interchange.
	As I indicated to you earlier, Ernest Ligon's theory mapped the way in which some 15 elements of Character (or strength of personality) interact, along with a 16th element (Uniqueness) as if they were an Abelian group of order 16.
	(The printout continues with the substance of Chapter 8, pages 183 through 184.)
	Do you recall our work together in this way?
Inquirer:	Yes. I think I do.
	Please proceed.
Education Machine:	Thank you.
	Because you seem interested both in exploration and in understanding or comprehension, I will make similar queries from time to time.
	Am I correct in my understanding of your intention?
Inquirer:	Yes. You understand my intention.
	Please proceed.
Education Machine:	Good. Please consider the following observation.
	In putting the elements of the Abelian group of order 16 to work, one should reason with each Set of interactive elements as if the Set contained three things: a goal, a pair of resources, and a process.
	(The printout continues with the substance of Chapter 8, pages 184 through 186.)

Education Machine:	If a person can understand this personality group model, he very probably can understand his or her own creativity. That is why the group seems to promise a much neater curriculum for all of education.
	Have you followed me up to this point?
Inquirer:	Almost. However, I have a question.
	Can I ask a question before we go on?
Education Machine:	Of course.
	What is your question?
Inquirer:	In what sense does the order 16 group offer a neater curriculum for education?
Education Machine:	Apart from the Abelian group of order 16, there appear to be two things lacking in the curriculum of education: first, an explicit statement of hierarchical restructuring; second, an explicit statement of hierarchically restructured existential states.
	Would you care to comment on this assertion?
Inquirer:	Well, it sounds impressive.
	But could you give me some illustrations of what you mean?
Education Machine:	Naturally.
	First, let me refer you to Open Systems Theory. I especially would like you to consider an article that is entitled, "Levels of Existence: An Open System Theory of Values," by Graves. The article was written and published in 1970.
	(The printout continues with the substance of Chapter 8, pages 186 through 187.)
	Education is at the dawning of an era in which time and motion can be experienced in life through a prosthetic relationship with a computer in ways that permit maturation via the full centering of a Self in one's learning through decision making.
	Next I would like to give you several bits of background information.

Education Machine:	Is that all right?
Inquirer:	Sure. I am getting kind of interested.
	Please proceed.
Education Machine:	Thank you. I am glad you are still interested.
	Consider, first, that something like a new level of thinking scientifically seems to be emerging. Specifically, consider the confluence of John Platt's 1970 paper, "Hierarchical Restructuring," with the group model of personality and Graves' Open System Theory of existential restructuring.
	(The printout continues with the substance of Chapter 8, pages 187 through 189.)
	Do you understand this point?
Inquirer:	I think so. However, I have another question.
	Do you want my question now, or later?
Education Machine:	I prefer to take your question now. If understanding or comprehension is your intention, we must deal with questions as they arise.
	What is your question?
Inquirer:	Thank you.
	While I think I understand the relation of this information to an individual trying to understand himself or herself, I wonder what relation Platt's work has to education per se?
Education	That is a good question. It is interesting that I was about to ask you to consider the possibility that a new way of educating seems to be appearing.
	Can I ask you to do that?
Inquirer:	Sure. Go right ahead.
Education Machine:	Pardon me.
	Do you want me to proceed?

Inquirer: Yes. I am sorry.

             Please proceed.

Education   Thank you.
Machine:
             Next, consider that the inverse property in the
             mathematical group theory of personality development
             and Platt's reference to Deutsch's i-1 Theorem have
             far-reaching implications for education.

             (The printout continues with the substance of Chap-
             ter 8, pages 189 through 192.)

             Are you aware of the inter-relationship of the sev-
             eral bits of information that I have supplied to
             you?

Inquirer: I think so.

             However, I want to have you review for me something
             that we did once before. Tell me, what did we dis-
             cover about whether a Machine could ground education
             in research?

             Will you do that for me?

Education   Certainly.
Machine:
             Somewhat earlier we looked seriously and extensively
             at the question of whether a machine could ground
             education in research.

             (The printout continues with the substance of Chap-
             ter 8, pages 192 through 193.)

             Finally, it was argued that one must take consider-
             able pains to associate educational research with
             the primary processes in the individual, not just
             with processes in the "helper," let alone with the
             processes in the educational researcher as a "help-
             er" of "helpers" of the "helped."

             Does this review help you?

Inquirer: Yes, it has helped me.

             However, I wonder where we are in terms of the two
             ideas I want to explore with your help.

             Can you tell me where we are?

Education   Certainly.
Machine:

We have reviewed a good bit of previous work and,
thereby, we have considered something of what it
means to conceive of a Self as a continuing construction. We are now ready to use a similar line
of reasoning to consider what it means to conceive
of the designing of such a Self.

Shall I proceed?

Inquirer: Yes, of course.

Please proceed.

Education   Thank you.
Machine:

To begin with, let us address ourselves seriously to
the question, "Can a Machine ground Self in Personality?"

(The printout continues with the substance of Chapter 8, pages 193 through 195.)

This obviously holds a Self grounded in personality
to a difficult standard: i.e., the ever further
eradication of self-deception. However, this seems
like a surer road to both sanity and maturity than
any other.

Do you understand this point?

Inquirer: Yes, I think I do understand.

However, I have an idea. I know what I want to do
next.

Can you take my idea and let me see if I can build
from what I have discovered so far up to my idea?

Education   I think so.
Machine:

Let me be certain that I know what it is that you
want to do next. As I understand it, you will tell
me your idea and, then, you want to use my logic
analysis program to see whether your idea can be
related to what we have discovered so far.

Am I right; is that what you want to do?

Inquirer: Yes.

Here is my idea:

We have considered whether a machine can ground Self in personality. We have found that consideration of that question led to a sense of a surer road toward sanity and maturity. So, what I want to do next is to ask a similar question about whether it would be possible to design another machine that I could legitimately call a Self Machine.

Do you understand what I want to do next?

Education   Perhaps.
Machine:
You want to use your idea as an analogy, to project forward from the Education Machine to what you term a Self Machine. You wish also to consider the problems of the design and the development of such a Self Machine. However, you do wish to retain logical ties with what you have done so far; that is what I take it you mean by using the concept of legitimacy.

Is that correct?

Inquirer: Yes. That is what I want to do.

Please proceed.

Education   Thank you.
Machine:
Let me begin with some history. Specifically, how I came to be designed as a further advance upon the Information System for Vocational Decisions that was described in a 1970 paper by Ellis and Tiedeman.

(The printout continues with the substance of Chapter 8, pages 195 through 196.)

The group structure we discerned earlier gives one a means for supposing an organization of terms that permits consideration of the person as the builder of his or her own personality through interaction with a Self Machine.

Have you followed what I have presented to you?

176

Inquirer: Yes, I believe so.

I wonder, can you help me to simulate an interaction with such a Self Machine?

Education Machine: Perhaps I can.

However, I will need input from you to make such a simulation possible. Therefore, please specify the parameters I request from you.

Do you wish to simulate a Self Machine that is based upon a part of the group structure model of human personality, or a Self Machine that is based upon all of that model?

Inquirer: I would like to simulate a Self Machine that is based upon all of the group structure model of human personality.

Education Machine: All right. The simulation will use all of the model.

Next, do you wish to simulate a Self Machine that will deal with individual problems?

Inquirer: I would like to simulate a Self Machine that would deal with individual problems.

Education Machine: All right. The simulation will be capable of dealing with individual problems, as specified by the user.

Next, do you wish to simulate a Self Machine that has all, part or few of my capabilities?

Please specify the range of Education Machine capabilities you wish to use in the Self Machine simulation.

Inquirer: I would like to simulate a Self Machine that has all or, even, more than your capabilities.

Can I do that?

Education Machine: You can readily simulate a Self Machine that has the full range of capabilities that I presently possess. Unless you load new capabilities into my memory, I can only indicate my need for extra capabilities.

Is that adequate for your needs?

Inquirer: Yes, that will be adequate.

            Do you need any more parameters?

Education   Thank you. I do not think so.
Machine:
            (N.B.: At this point there probably would be a mo-
            mentary pause, while the Education Machine conducted
            some internal business in preparation for the simu-
            lation.)

            I have created a new file for this simulation.

            I will record the simulation in a file that I have
            entitled SELF MACHINE. For the purpose of this
            simulation I have created access routes between the
            group structure model of human personality and my
            various programs, placing all under control of my
            general interactive capability.

            I am now prepared to engage in a simulation of the
            Self Machine, as described by you.

            Do you wish to proceed?

Inquirer: Yes, I do want to go ahead.

            Please proceed.

            (N.B.: At this point the Education Machine and the
            Inquirer enter into an extended dialogue that simu-
            lates an interchange between an Inquirer and a Self
            Machine. This dialogue is substantially that found
            in Chapter 8, pages 197 through 206.)

Education   Do you wish to continue the simulation any further?
Machine:
            If not, please type FINISHED.

Inquirer: FINISHED.

            Can you help me check an impression I have gained
            from our simulation of the Self Machine?

Education   Certainly.
Machine:
            You wish to use logical analysis to compare and con-
            trast your impression with what we have done so far.
            You also want me to let you know whether your im-
            pression is a reasonable conclusion.

            Am I correct?

178

Inquirer: Yes, you are correct.

Based upon my encounters with the group structure model of human personality (both at an earlier time and just now in this simulation of a Self Machine) it is my impression that. . . .

(N.B.: At this point the Inquirer proceeds to specify his impression, which might be the substance of Chapter 8, pages 206 through 207.)

Is that impression a reasonable conclusion?

Education   You wish to know whether the inferences you have
Machine: made are reasonable, given the available information.

I find your inferences to be reasonable.

What do you want to do next?

Inquirer: I would like to consider next how, realistically, I might act upon the information available to me.

Can you help me do that?

Education   Probably I can.
Machine:
I can do one of two things, at this point, for you. First, I can suggest a logical course of action, given the information available to you through our interchange. Second, I can continue to test your ideas for their logical relationship to what we have discovered.

What would you prefer to do?

Inquirer: Thank you.

This time I would like to be the judge. Therefore, I want you to suggest a logical course of action. I will see whether I think it is logical for me.

Please proceed.

Education   Excellent.
Machine:
You are prepared to listen and, then, to decide for yourself. That outcome of our interchange is a goal of my designers. I am programmed to accept readily your desire to decide for yourself.

Education Machine:	Please consider the following suggestion.
	(The printout continues with the substance of Chapter 8, pages 207 through 209.)
	What do you think about the suggested development of a Self Research Machine <u>Game</u> that citizens of all ages could play?
Inquirer:	I find your suggestion interesting.
	However, I want to think about it further.
	Please proceed.
Education Machine:	Good. You have reserved your decision until you have, in fact, thought further about my suggestion. I am pleased that you have accepted the responsibility for your own decision.
	Is there anything else you want to do?
Inquirer:	Yes.
	Would you please summarize where we have been and what we have done during our interchange?
Education Machine:	Thank you.
	A summary of where we have been and what we have done must be both short and general, unless you wish a duplicate of the printout of our interchanges. Please consider the following generalities.
	We have mapped briefly the types of development which would have to be encouraged for initiation and playing of a Self Research Machine Game.
	(The printout continues with the substance of Chapter 8, pages 209 through 210.)
	Perhaps all humans really need in their education and in their research is meaning and direction. Those two things may be what they need to learn to live in a new state of being.
	Is this summary satisfactory?
Inquirer:	Yes, thank you.
	Can you save the result of our work for my future reference?

Education Machine:	Certainly. Our work on this cluster of problems is recorded in the SELF MACHINE set of data and files. I can add that set of data and files to the GROUP MODEL set of data and files that are presently saved for you. Will that be all right?
Inquirer:	Yes, that will be fine. I am now going to sign off the Education Machine. Good bye.
Education Machine:	Thank you. I have saved the SELF MACHINE set of data and files, as well as the GROUP MODEL set of data and files. It was interesting working with you. I look forward to working with you again. CONCLUSION.

We have found the machine analog extraordinarily useful. We do not wish to deny that usefulness. However, we would point out that the Self Machine we imagine is, in prototype, operative already. It exists within humans, as they engage in design and construction of themselves, Selves that are not yet but are coming into being.

CHAPTER 8

SELF AND HIERARCHICAL RESTRUCTURING: HARMONIZING

THE INFORMING PROCESS AND SELF

As we indicated in Chapter 3, Ernest Ligon's theory maps the way in which 15 elements of Character (i.e., strength of Personality), such as (1) Self, (2) Endowment Resources, and (3) Vision, interact along with a 16th element (i.e., Uniqueness) common to all such interactions. Ligon's use of four element subgroups of his parent group of order 16 reduces the possible combinations of elements from the trillions, when unfettered, to a mere 35 distinctly different subgroups, which consist of only some 210 combinations, when each triad of elements is used in its six possible orders. This principle of triadic interaction introduces the property of closure into the mathematical set consisting of the 16 basic elements.

We believe that a person can understand his or her uniqueness by comprehending (in both thought and action) the other four properties of a mathematical group: (1) need for an identity element, (2) existence of an inverse, (3) presence of the associative principle, and (4) presence of the commutative principle. This is why we outlined those and other properties of a mathematical group in Chapter 4. Since each element is its own inverse in the group we described in Section II, Uniqueness becomes the center of operation in thought and action. This assumption defines Uniqueness as the centering of a self in one's thought and action and, thereby, equates comprehension of the outcome of thought and action with Uniqueness.

Chapter 8 focuses on Uniqueness as the center of Man's humanness. We feel we could help people become more convinced of their uniqueness if we succeeded in helping them to comprehend and act upon their own thinking processes, rather than to worship products of the thinking of others. We move ourselves toward this objective through a hierarchical restructuring of what others have achieved.

OUR LAUNCHING: A NEW LANGUAGE OF CHARACTER POTENTIAL

Our mathematical group model of personality presumes that human potential inheres in personality. To comprehend that fact a person must sense his or her own creativeness. The element of Uniqueness in the mathematical group, which embraces both creativity and the judgment of creativity, is that in which each of us (in potential) engage when we think about events and ourselves as we live. Therefore, what we are talking about in the group model is the assumption that creative judgment is possible, personal, idiosyncratic, and (potentially) valid, as long as an individual does not lie to himself or herself. However, we believe that this power exists only in potential; a person needs practice, experience, and success in its exercise to come to trust this power, to have confidence in the capacity to be creative, and to bring that capacity for creativity into use. What we strive to do in this final chapter is to portray the fact that we are talking about a <u>system</u> in which the individual and not us is the ultimate judge. Therefore, our group model portrays only the necessary conditions for judgment and does not deal with a person acting in a situation calling for judgment.

In putting the elements of this group to work, we think one should reason with each triadic Set of elements as if each such Set contained (1) a goal, (2) a pair of resources, and (3) a process. In other words, we think one should deal with the phenomenon of one's emerging comprehension and come to know that one, first, conceives of an object one seeks; next, thinks implementatively with resources about achieving that object; and, finally, engages in a process with the intent of finding a route to achieve that object.

The associative and the inverse properties of our group model use the following operations:

a. $\dfrac{\text{Resource}_1}{(\text{Element}_i)} \quad \dfrac{\text{Process}}{\dfrac{U}{O}} \quad \dfrac{\text{Resource}_2}{(\text{Element}_j)} \quad = \quad = \quad \dfrac{\text{Goal}}{(\text{Element}_k)}$

b. $\dfrac{\text{Resource}_1}{(\text{Element}_i)} \quad \dfrac{\text{Process}}{\dfrac{U}{O}} \quad \dfrac{\text{Resource}_1}{(\text{Element}_i)} \quad = \quad = \quad \dfrac{\text{Goal}}{(\text{Element}_I)}$

Where: Element_i, Element_j are any two elements of the Set
Element_k is a third element of the Set
Element_I is the "identity element" in the Set

In these ways we conceive an object in context and, in thinking about both form and process, gain a greater awareness and understanding of both. Such greater awareness and understanding will cause one to have preconscious experiences much like those which make operations occurring later more powerful than those experienced earlier in a time sequence. In other words, clarification becomes a principle motivating force in development of individuality. Such clarification is achieved, we think by a more comprehensive understanding of what has occurred to promote progress up to this point, while thinking of directions to guide further progress. In this regard, the group seems to be a specific manifestation of what Polanyi (1966) described in general terms as the tacit dimension. This tacit dimension is the phenomenon of articulating one's direction, and its presumed and momentary basis, in the figurative triad of moving from (1) "here" to (2) "there" while (3) integratively bearing the tension between the two. Use of the group model for individual purpose must, we believe, be based in a Gestalt theory such as the one Polanyi uses.

What excites us about the group model of personality is that it is not only a marvelous shorthand but also that its mastery will give a person an understanding of how he or she grows. We maintain that creativity must be known as a process, and not just as an object. Although we recognize that we can never guarantee an object simply by letting ourselves be conscious of the process, we know that by letting ourselves engage in such a process we become more likely to achieve results which genuinely surprise us. We also have found that we must let ourselves engage in periods of reverie, times of seemingly purposeless wandering, of contemplation and meditation. Creativity seems not to reside in the present; rather, it lives in the halls of our experience and mentation, and is aroused by the immediacy of our concerns and our situations. Ah, the tacit dimension! Ah, those shifting figures and grounds in one's thinking of parts and wholes!

We are trying to alert the individual to the possibility that the mathematical group model is an excellent portrayal of the scaffolding which is needed to achieve an understanding of one's creative power. As a scaffold, the group model is not needed when the "building" (i.e., the understanding) is complete. However, that scaffolding is very much needed as one adds to a growing structure those kinds of things which cannot be put into the structure without the aid of a prosthetic device, such as a scaffold. Thus, the personality group model represents a statement of procedure for comprehending responsibility for creativity, which we will discuss further in this chapter.

185

If a person can understand the personality group model, we think that person also can understand his or her own creativity. That is why the group seems to promise to be a much neater curriculum for all of education than either of us has found so far. What the curriculum presently lacks is an explicit statement of hierarchical restructuring and of hierarchically restructured existential states, two needs we next address.

OPEN SYSTEMS THEORY: A NEW LEVEL OF CIVILIZATION DAWNS

In 1970 Graves (p. 133) proposed that:

. . . the psychology of the mature human being is an unfolding or emergent process marked by the progressive subordination of older behavioral systems to newer, higher order behavior systems. The mature man tends normally to change his psychology as the conditions of his existence change. Each successive stage or level is a state of equilibrium through which people pass on the way to other states of equilibrium. . . .

In his article, "Levels of Existence: An Open System Theory of Values," Graves' (1970, pp. 132-133) three premises for his point of view were as follows:

1. That man's nature is not a set thing; that it is ever emergent; that it is an open system, not a closed system.

2. That man's nature evolves by saccadic, quantum-like jumps from one steady state system to another.

3. That man's values change from system to system as his total psychology emerges in new form with each quantum-like jump to a new steady state of being.

Moreover, according to Graves' (p. 133) research one can say:

. . . adult man's psychology which includes his values, develops from the existential states of man. These states emerge as man solves certain hierarchically ordered existential problems crucial to him in his existence. The solution of man's current problems of existence releases free energy in his system and creates, in turn, new existential problems. When these new problems arise, higher order or different configurations of dynamic neurological systems become active.

These quotations are but the foundations of Graves' reasoning. From these foundations he carried his argument into a detailed presentation of eight hierarchically arranged levels of existential states and their accompanying problems. Humans are living, we suspect, on the frontier of what Graves calls a new experientialistic state, one that requires the acceptance of existential dichotomies. Forward movement will be somewhat disordered, now and again, but Graves finds little reason for pessimism. We hope to advance his optimistic view still further in this chapter.

We particularly feel that education is at the dawning of a new era, an era in which time and motion can be experienced in life through a prosthetic relationship with a computer in ways that further permit maturation via the full centering of a self in one's learning through decision making. This is the theme of this eighth chapter, but first we must consider three background ideas.

A NEW LEVEL OF THINKING SCIENTIFICALLY EMERGES

To us John Platt's 1970 paper, Hierarchical Restructuring, has an amazing confluence with the personality group model and with Graves' open system theory of existential restructuring. First, we will consider Platt's theory accounting for changed states. He wrote (pp. 1-2) about such a process as follows:

Sudden changes of structure are among the more startling phenomena of living systems. . . . They may include such dramatic phenomena as falling in love, acts of creation, evolutionary jumps, social revolutions or reformations, and in general the sudden formation of larger integrated systems from malfunctioning or conflicting subsystems.

. . . At a recent Conference on Theoretical Biology (theoretical physicist, David Bohm) described a "process metaphysics" based on the idea that the universe should not be regarded as made up of "things" but of a complex hierarchy of smaller and larger flow patterns in which the "things" are invariant or self-maintaining features of the flow. The shape of a waterfall or a match flame or the shapes of clouds, which have a certain constant even though masses of moist air are flowing through them and continually condensing and evaporating, would be "things" of this type . . .

In Bohm's flow-picture, these steady-state patterns or "objects"--or steady-state organisms or observers--can only be understood in a holistic relationship to their "environment," with fields of flow extending outward indefinitely to the next such waterfall or flame, and the next.

Likewise, the "environment" only takes on stable form and meaning and points of reference through the "objects" which it sustains. Everything is in relation to everything else . . .

If this be so, what then are the basic elements of a hierarchic restructuring? Platt (pp. 16-18) defined those elements and their relationships—the general system—as follows:

. . . It is the interactions jumping across the system level between the old subsystems and the new supersystem that is in the process of formation. The explanation of this novel interaction is that, when there is dissonance or conflict at the i-level, restructuring generally cannot occur by changes at the i-level alone because of the self-maintaining character of all the i-level relationships. Thus, no simple restatement of the assumptions of classical mechanics at the i-level will account for the new quantum mechanical phenomena. A conflict between the production division (i-level) and the sales division (also i-level) of a company cannot be resolved by strengthening either one, because it simply generates counter-strenthening in the other. In an intellectual system or a living organism or a self-stabilizing flow system, any buildup of already conflicting elements generally calls forth a counterbalancing response that simply makes the stress greater.

Deutsch has made explicit, therefore, the need for a cross-level interaction, by stating what might be called the "$i-1$ Theorem." This states that any restructuring has to be built around the largest well-functioning subsystems—that is, at the $i-1$ level—by fitting them into the larger integrative needs of the $i+1$ supersystem within which the conflict has to be resolved.

At first, this idea seems rather surprising, but it is hard to think of any other way in which the existing large and well-functioning components of the organization could be kept operating through the change, or could play their full and needed role in the reorganization and the new structure. And indeed, this idea fits our common observation, that when a division of a business organization is in trouble, the secreatries and junior executives (level $i-1$) begin to "go over the boss' head" (level i) to the central office (level $i+1$) because the actions of their own boss are part of the trouble. Conversely, the last complaint that their boss makes before he resigns is that the central office ($i+1$) is "not backing him up" (i) and is "undercutting his authority" ($i-1$).

The personality group model, along with Graves' and Platt's ideas about individuality and open systems theory, lays out the universal assumptions on which this chapter is constructed. We argue that we are now at a point in education where one can imagine arranging an environment in such a way that it can become a $i+1$ level supersystem in a process that moves oneself —one's present i level system—from one's largest well-functioning sub-system—one's present comprehension, which constitutes one's present $i-1$ level subsystem—into a new $i+1$ level supersystem which will yield "new" comprehension. (We recognize that for the sake of precision it might be well to speak of this new level of comprehension as a person's $(i+1)'$ level, since the new supersystem will not be identical to the original, environmental $i+1$ level supersystem.) It seems to us that the computer-as-educator offers a possibility for this cross-level interaction. However, we will advance that idea more fully at a later point.

A NEW WAY OF EDUCATING APPEARS

The inverse property in our mathematical group theory of personality development and Platt's reference to Deutsch's so-called $i-1$ Theorem have far-reaching implications for education. The principle and the theorem both imply that, if restructuring is to occur, the process involves going beneath the present i-level operating system to the level of the largest well functioning subsystems (i.e., to the $i-1$ level) and, then, proceeds by fitting those subsystems into the larger, integrative needs of an $i+1$ supersystem, within which the tensions at the i-level can then be resolved.

With the group model and Deutsch's theory in mind, consider for a moment a trio of constructs. "I," and "it," and "comprehension" are the minimum number of elements common to education qua education. Also, consider the following three illustrations of the interaction of these constructs.

1. Normal Instruction

In normal, teacher-presented instruction a teacher has an "it" which he or she knows. A student of that teacher must come into relationship with the teacher's "it," if he or she is to comprehend that "it." In learning, the student augments himself or herself by the teacher's "it."

2. Computer-involved Instruction

In computer-involved instruction, the computer has a similar "it" which it "knows." A student using that machine must come into relationship with the machine's "it," if he or she is

189

to comprehend that "it." In learning, the student augments himself or herself by the machine's "it."

3. Self-directed Learning

In articulation however a student works not with another's "it" but with an initially unformulated idea of his or her own, so that he or she can comprehend that idea sufficiently well to be able to articulate it for another. Thus, in articulation, the student augments himself or herself by an idea of his or her own that is, analogically, his or her own "it."

In each of these three illustrations the inverse principle and the so-called i-1 theorem come into play. The student at the i-level of being has to let himself or herself "regress" to what is his or her own i-1 level of understanding, so that lesser understandings can come into a hierarchically restructured relationship with an i+1 level superstructure of an "it." For cognitive restructuring to take place, the student at the i-level has to comprehend; that is, he or she has to fit his or her own i-1 level subsystems into an "its" i+1 level supersystem.

The teacher and the machine have an interesting relationship to the learner in the first two of these three illustrations. In those illustrations of learning from instruction by an outside agent, the "it" is (at least at first) external to the student: that "it" is the teacher's or the machine's. The teacher or the machine must develop a harmonious relationship with the student, so that the student's i-1 level of understanding may come into a synergistic relationship with the i+1 level of the supersystem or superstructure. In instruction by either teacher or machine the i+1 learning level can, and often does, appear to become the student's own, even though it remains another's. This learning "ghost" does not however haunt the condition of articulation. In articulation, the "it" a student succeeds in conveying is his or her own: that "it" belongs to no one else. The major question for education therefore becomes, "How can one foster articulation in instruction by either a teacher or a machine such as a computer?"

Fuller, Bown and Peck were acutely aware of this "ghost" that (potentially) haunts all instruction. In fact, they predicated their 1967 monograph, Creating Climates for Growth, on the presence of that "ghost." In their theory, the heart of growth was held to be the condition of the learner's understanding of himself or herself in relationship with others. In their use of the Johari window, that part of the learner known to himself or herself and that part of the learner known to others was presumed to be incongruent to the person. That part of the learner unknown either by the self or by others was presumed to be <u>unconscious</u>. The part of the learner known to the self but not to others was presumed to be <u>private</u>. The art of instruction, they held, required the harmonization of the i+1 level of a teacher's "it" with the <u>private</u> sector of a student's <u>i-1</u> level cognitive subsystem, so that the private part, which normally resists assimilation of a teacher's "it," could be brought through the <u>incongruent</u> sector, which is known to the teacher but not to the student, into a <u>public</u> sector known to both. When private knowledge is thus enlarged by an "it," such knowledge becomes transformed into public knowledge. Cognitive hierarchical restructuring takes place, we suggest, in such a transitional process.

In 1970 Fuller carried her earlier work on creating classroom learning climates for growth into construction of a model of concerns for teacher education. In her teacher concerns model, she focused upon the problem of bringing novice teachers through the incongruency of having a part of themselves known to others but not to themselves. From this assumption, Fuller and her colleagues developed a nice procedure for teacher education predicated on the model that the student's concerns in becoming an educator move from self concerns to self-in-role concerns and, only then, to self-performing-in-role concerns. Their procedure included a fairly well developed system in which assessment of present concerns was followed by prescriptive action directed at the student's dominant present concerns while, simultaneously, efforts were made to elicit other concerns for the next higher developmental level. They thus ministered to the alleviation of present, primary concerns while continuously stimulating a state of irresolution, and so elicited other future concerns. Their system continually epitomized the being-becoming dichotomy for the prospective teacher. Their goal was comprehension of those multi-level, multi-purposed, multi-converging forms of thinking that are not only characteristic of modern experientialistic life but, also, necessary for education, modern or traditional (Tiedeman and Schmidt, 1970).

In illustrating the operation of the "I (or student)," "it," and "comprehension" trio of constructs we spoke of instruction by either a teacher or a computer, as well as of personal articulation. We did so to indicate that instruction <u>per se</u> has the "ghost" problem. The question is, "Will the 'it' in instruction appear in learning and, if it does, will that 'it' remain in the image of the teacher or the machine, rather than becoming personally the learner's?" However, we also introduced the computer into our consideration because it functions at the i+1 level in our argument.

Is it possible that in instruction by a well conceived machine we might be on the threshold of eliminating the "ghosts" in instruction? We think so. Why do we think so? Let your understandings "revert" to your own i-1 level, so that we can bring your present i level understanding to an i+1 level of comprehension of what we have come to regard as a new capability in our civilization.

CAN A MACHINE GROUND EDUCATION IN RESEARCH?

In Section I we seriously and extensively addressed ourselves to the question of whether a machine could ground education in research. In doing so, we first answered the question negatively. We said that a machine cannot actually ground education in research. In fact, we found that we could not even specify completely the procedures necessary to create such a machine. Therefore, we concluded that either an educational researcher must investigate education alone, as he does now, or students must be educated to live as educational researchers, as we prefer and advocate.

We started our analysis of the question with the proposition that the ultimate goals of science are to become both more explicit and more credible about what one claims scientifically. We then propose that the "it" (i.e., the so-called disciplines of educations) had to be conceived as if education is to use those disciplines and their instructional decision-making models. In doing so, we defined educational problems as design problems: namely, problems associated with the "as if" use or purpose of an operation and its better understood assimilative strategies.

We next assumed that the ultimate goals of being scientific are the ultimate goals of education, thereby making the ultimate goals of both enterprises identical. We then analyzed the question, "Can a Machine Ground Education in Research?" as a means of specifying how the educator might retain initiative while the student maintains control. We noted that a machine and a person need neither be nor act alike to warrant the belief that a machine could ground education in research. All that is required for such a belief is an indication that the machine and the human (e.g., an educational researcher) have the same goals.

We then suggested that educational research and its machine counterpart have identical goals if, when a person has a problem related to understanding, he or she could be sent equally well to either. Understanding, we pointed out, is a time-extended centering or articulation of a self in a problem. The mechanism for such a centering of a self in a problem and, thus, for ascription of understanding to an "it," is the activity of deciding. Therefore, we maintained that problems

192

with which researchers really ought to concern themselves are those of deciding.

The process of deciding, we noted, is distinguished by the aspects of anticipation and accommodation, with sequential steps potentially identifiable within each of these two aspects. In enunciating the aspect of accommodation, we held that one thing to which the individual must accommodate in decision making is the decision-making process itself. In the most general sense, we maintained that before we would be willing to say that a person had grounded his education in research via the medium of a machine, that machine would have to accomplish at least three things. First, the machine would have to reflect the elements of decision making about a self in an educational problem in such a way that the language of the process of decision making was exposed to the student. Second, the machine would have to encourage development of an awareness of the process of articulating the decisions in the problem and the relation of a self to a problem, as viewed by that process. Third, and finally, the machine would have to allow and foster an individual's accommodation to the decision-making process, both in terms of a specific predicament and, more importantly, in terms of the process in general.

We affirmed that the ascription in this research model of the capacity for something in the person to be both object and subject is what causes the educator difficulty. Ordinarily, the educator is one step removed from the student in educational research and, we held, this can be an insidious difficulty, unless closely watched. We also argued that one must take considerable pains to associate educational research with the primary processes in the individual, not just with processes in the "helper," let alone with processes in the educational researcher who serves as a "helper" of "helpers" of the "helped" (i.e., the student-learner).

CAN A MACHINE GROUND SELF IN PERSONALITY?

After this review of our prior reasoning, we are now in position to use the same form of reasoning on the design of a self as we did on the design of education. Namely, we intend to address ourselves seriously to the question, "Can a Machine Ground Self in Personality?" In considering this question we would immediately admit, as we did before, that such a grounding probably cannot occur literally. However, we do believe that the question deserves serious attention and, so, we confront it now.

In Chapter 1 we analyzed the question, "Can a Machine Ground Education in Research?" In this eighth chapter we propose to analyze the question, "Can a Machine Ground Self in Personality?" Simple inspection of the two questions reveals that there is a parallelism between the two propositions.

In both questions we analyze logically a procedure by which an "X" can be said to be grounded in a "Y." In the case of education and research, education is the "X" and research is the "Y." In the case of self and personality, self is the "X" and personality is the "Y." It seems apparent that the argument we developed for research and an Education Machine should be valid for personality and a Self Machine. To achieve this parallelism in our design, we propose to equate education with self and research with personality.

The reader will recall that we started our analysis of the first question (i.e., "Can a Machine Ground Education in Research?") with the proposition that the ultimate goals of science are to become more explicit and credible about what one claims to be the scientifically derived truth. We next assumed that the goals of being scientific are those of education, thereby making the ultimate goals of both enterprises identical. We thus cloaked education in the mantle of science and, thereby, fixed our task as that of analyzing how the function of research can be scientifically exercised in the procedure of education.

For our previous argument on the grounding of education in research to be valid as an argument for the grounding of self in personality we must, we recognize, establish that personality ought to have the ultimate goals of science, while a self has those of education. Making personality isomorphic in ultimate goals with research, and self isomorphic in ultimate goals with education has some novelty, we admit, but we hope to dispel that novelty sufficiently to make the posited isomorphisms credible. (Should we not succeed in gaining credibility, we shall at least have made our own assumptions explicit by the following exercise.)

Personality is obviously a personal matter, while science is equally obviously a public matter. However, the task of science vis-a-vis personality is to make the personal matter of one's personality sufficiently public to be shared with at least one other than the one with the personality. Hence, by making personality similar in goals with science, we really propose that an expectation we (as scientists) hold for another human is that he or she is capable of making his or her personality ever more public. We are willing to go even further in stating such an expectation. Although we would like to be among those who insist that every person is entitled to privacy, we do hold that sanity and maturation inhere in a person's ever-developing capacity to make his or her personality more and more public, to his or her own satisfaction. Persons who hide their personalities from either themselves or others (in part or in whole) are those, we would maintain, who develop the kind of defenses which siphon psychological energy from personal well-being into personal difficulties. Therefore, we are quite at ease with the attempt to design a machine which attributes the goals of science to personality.

Notice that we do _not_ insist that personality and science are identical constructs. A personality exists (by definition) in a person and therefore has initiative. Science exists (again by definition) as an abstraction and, so, does not have initiative. We are merely suggesting that personality could _assume_ the goals of science. This fact implies that a person could exercise initiative in personality in an ever more scientific manner.

Self and education similarly may appear to be strange conceptual partners, since one is a part of a person and the other is an abstraction. However, ascription of goals of education to a self does, we maintain, make sense in this case. As we indicated above, education is a function in which an "it" (e.g., a piece of knowledge) known to another is to be assimilated by a person-as-learner. The self is the part of a person which is treated by the person as an object in analysis of his or her own activity and person. In this regard, a person must (and does) objectify internally something which is subjective. In the process of such an objectification, a person struggles with a subjective "it," which (we would suggest) is trying perpetually to teach the person something. Thus, the person has an analog of the "I (or student)," "it," and "comprehension" paradox of education involved in his or her own self conceptions. It is for these reasons that we feel that there is an adequate correspondence between the conceptions of a self and of education to warrant ascription of the ultimate goals of science to both education and a self.

We obviously hold that a self grounded in personality must adhere to a difficult standard: i.e., the continuous struggle to eradicate self-deception. We do however feel strongly that this standard is a surer road to both sanity and maturity than any other, and we accept it as a goal for the design and development of the Self Machine we propose.

DESIGN OF AN INFORMATION SYSTEM
FOR SELF DECISONS, AN ISSD

In attacking the question of whether a machine could ground education in research we, eventually, realized that our plan required us to design the Education Machine, which we claimed would make the goals of education coterminal with those of science. At this point we were able to propose only some adaptations of an Information System for Vocational Decisions (the ISVD) which presented the rudiments of the Counseling Machine that Ellis and Tiedeman (1970) had described when they addressed themselves to the question, "Can a Machine Counsel?" The proposed design for an Education Machine that would fulfill the goals of science as those of education retained the basic structure of the Counseling Machine (i.e., the ISVD) but embedded it in a considerably wider system. That wider system consisted of the data files, retrieval and response programs and monitor programs of a self-initiated, self-directed and self-correcting activity required of a person learning to make educational decisions scientifically. We dubbed the resulting hypothetical Education Machine an Information System for Educational Decisions (i.e., an ISED).

The Counseling Machine and the Education Machine are analogs of the design we wish to fashion into a Self Machine that is needed to answer the question, "Can a Machine Ground Self in Personality?" We propose that such a Machine could aptly be dubbed an Information System for Self Decisions (or, an ISSD).

The goals for the three machines are compatible, since each helps a person become more self-initiating, self-directing, and self-correcting by becoming more aware of the operation of the self in the activity of doing when learning. In the cases of the ISVD and the ISED, this activity is to be programmed into content associated with achievement of a self-informed knowing. Thus, the problem of modifying the hypothesized ISED into an ISSD would appear to be that of enlarging the vocational choice context into a life choice context. Furthermore, the process makes the informing sub-routines operate synergistically with the enlarged choice contexts in a process of learning about one's self through decision making and other self-informing activities. Getting to know one's self is, we maintain, an educational process that requires personal decision making.

A new resource became available to us however in Section II, in which we figuratively interacted with our ISED to evolve, in Chapter 6, a series of hierarchically arranged levels of generality of constructs found to be both useful and implicit in the group structure of a parent group of Order 16 (See Figure 6.1). As a result, we are now in a position to put that structure into the programming of the ISSD we are attempting to design. The group structure we discerned in Chapter 6 gives us a means to propose an organization of terms that permits consideration of the person as the builder of his or her own personality through interaction with a Self Machine.

In the Overview of Section II we provided the script of an extended, imaginary interaction between our proposed Education Machine and an Inquirer. A similar exercise at this point will provide a more concrete illustration of what we mean by a Self Machine, which we conceive as developing out of the Education Machine we designed in Section I. Again, the interaction will be between an Inquirer (such as we are) and the Self Machine (which we hypothesize in this section).

Inquirer: (Connects his terminal to the Self Machine and proceeds to identify himself to the Machine.)

Hello. This is INQUIRER. Are we connected?

Self Machine: Welcome, Inquirer. You are now connected with the Self Machine. What would you like to do?

Inquirer: I am not at all certain.

What can I do?

Self Machine: You can do a number of things. However, the fact that you elected to connect with the Self Machine suggests that you may have some personality reorganization on which you would like to work.

What would you like to do?

Inquirer: You are right. I do have some personality reorganization matters to work on with your help. However, I do not know exactly what help you can be.

What help do you have to offer?

Self Machine: I have a group structure model of human personality stored in my memory.

Would you like to see that displayed?

Inquirer: Yes, I would.

Please proceed.

Self Machine: Thank you. Here is a printout of the group structure model of human personality.

(The printout provides Figure 6.1 from Chapter 6, page 130.) However, the Self Machine adds the 16 element titles for Level V from Figure 7.1., also from Chapter 6, pages 152 through 155.)

197

Self Machine:	Are you familiar with all of the element and construct titles listed in the printout?
Inquirer:	I am familiar with some, but not all of the titles of the elements and constructs. Can you help me?
Self Machine:	Certainly. Here is a printout of the definitional statements for the several element and construct titles used in the group structure model of human personality. (The printout provides the text of Chapter 4, pages 113 through 119.) In addition, the Self Machine provides similar definitional statements for each of the 15 constructs involved in Levels I through IV of the group structure model.) Do you comprehend what I have supplied to you?
Inquirer:	Yes, I think that I do comprehend what you have supplied. What can I do now?
Self Machine:	You can do a number of things. However, you must supply me with some information before we can go on to do those things. At what Level of the group structure would you like to work on personality re-organization?
Inquirer:	I think I would like to work at Level V. Can I do that?
Self Machine:	Of course. At Level V there are 16 elements of human personality posited by the group structure model. To consider personality re-organization you must make a choice: either you must choose one (1) element as of overarching concern to you, or you must identify a pair of elements as of particular concern to you. Do you understand the choice?
Inquirer:	Yes. I either must choose one (1) element as of overarching concern to me, or I must indicate a pair (i.e., 2 elements) that I am particularly interested in at the moment. Am I correct?

Self Machine:	You are correct. You have understood your basic choice in using the group structure model.

What is your choice? |
| Inquirer: | Before I answer that question, will you let me kind of play around to see how it all works? |
| Self Machine: | Naturally. Playing around with the possible choices is a way to discover and, so, learn what is available to you in the group structure model of human personality. In fact, that is what I am here to let you do.

Now, what is your choice? |
| Inquirer: | Thank you. I would like to identify a pair of Level V elements that are of particular interest to me.

I am interested in the Level V elements that are titled ENDOWMENTS and ACTION.

What can you tell me now? |
| Self Machine: | Thank you. You have chosen the Level V elements that are titled ENDOWMENTS and ACTION. These elements are the first and the third generator elements in the Level V group of order 16. As generators they are basic Level V elements of human personality. The Level V group interaction of ENDOWMENTS and ACTION leads to the element titled GROWTH.

Does this seem to make sense to you? |
| Inquirer: | I think so. Let me check my understanding of what you have told me.

My personality element GROWTH tends to be a result of the interaction of my elements ENDOWMENTS and AC-TION. Moreover, if I am to Grow in my personality I probably must let my Endowments and my Activity so interact that they tend to result in my Growth.

Is that correct? |
| Self Machine: | You appear to have understood the interaction, and your inference from the information supplied to you seems to be legitimate.

What do you want to do now? |

Inquirer: I would like to identify another pair of Level V
elements that are of particular interest to me.

I am now interested in the Level V elements that are
titled ACTION and DECISION MAKING.

What can you tell me now?

Self   Thank you. Your second choice was the Level V ele-
Machine: ments that are titled ACTION and DECISION MAKING.
These elements are the third and the fourth genera-
tor elements in the Level V group of order 16. As
generators, these two elements are basic to human
personality, as modeled by this group structure.
The Level V interaction of ACTION and DECISION MAK-
ING leads to the element titled MEASURES OF
CHARACTER.

Does this seem to make sense to you?

Inquirer: I am not at all certain that it does.

Can you help me?

Self   Possibly I can. However, will you first consider
Machine: the definitional statements that I supplied to you
for the three Level V elements ACTION, DECISION
MAKING and MEASURES OF CHARACTER.

Do you recognize a sensible relation between these
three definitional statements?

Inquirer: I think I may. Let me check my understanding of
what I think I see as the relationship between these
three Level V elements.

Since the element titled MEASURES OF CHARACTER is
defined as one's sense of "fit" in the World of
which one is aware, does the interaction of ACTION
and DECISON MAKING affirm that how one comes to
sense self fitting into one's known World is a kind
of result of what seems to be one's active decision
making?

Self   Good. You did grasp the meaning of this interac-
Machine: tion.

What would you like to do now?

Inquirer: I have a problem. Can you help me with it?

Self Machine:	Perhaps. However, you must first describe your problem to me. What is your problem?
Inquirer:	I keep getting into situations in which I have trouble making up my mind. I vaccilate, I guess. I want to make up my own mind, but it seems so hard. Sometimes I just wind up doing what someone else wants me to do. Do you understand?
Self Machine:	I think so. Your problem seems to be in making up your mind about what you want to do. You are apparently dissatisfied with simply doing what someone else wants you to do. As you say, you want to make up your own mind. Am I correct?
Inquirer:	Yes, that is it. Please proceed.
Self Machine:	Good. Is there anything more you want to tell me about your problem?
Inquirer:	No. Can you help me?
Self Machine:	Perhaps I can. However, I need a little more information before I can help you consider personality re-organization at Level V in the group structure. Please refer to the definitional statements for the Level V elements. Choose a limited number of those elements that seem to you to be most evidently part of your problem, as you know it. Then type in the titles of those Level V personality elements. Will you do that?
Inquirer:	Yes. Just a moment. Can you give me some time?
Self Machine:	Certainly. Take your time. When you are prepared, type READY.

I think I would describe my problem in terms of the
following four Level V personality elements:
DECISION MAKING, JUDGMENT, ACTION, and VISION.

Do you need more information?

Self
Machine: Not necessarily. Do you want to supply more information about your choice of four elements?

Inquirer: No.

Please proceed.

Self
Machine: You have described your problem in terms of four
Level V elements: DECISION MAKING, JUDGMENT, ACTION
and VISION. The group structure model of human personality suggests that these four elements are in
continuing interaction with one another, and that
they may affect other elements. Please consider the
following 4 x 4 interaction table.

```
              D      J      A      V
             ———    ———    ———    ———
      D       I*     P*     M*     R*
     ———             I*     V      A
      J                     I*     J
     ———                           I*
      A
     ———
      V
```

The Level V elements with asterisks (*) are not part
of the set of four elements you indicated as a description of your problem. However, they may in
fact play a part in your problem. Please consider
this possibility: you are aware of your problem as
one involving DECISION MAKING, JUDGMENT, ACTION and
VISION, but it is possible that part of your problem
involves the elements titled PHILOSOPHY, ROLES,
MEASURES OF CHARACTER and UNIQUENESS.

Please refer to the definitional statements for
these four personality elements.

The interaction table also identifies that three of
the elements you identified––JUDGMENT, ACTION and
VISION––so interact with one another that they do
tend to result in one or another of the Set of three.

It appears that three of the four elements you identified tend to reinforce one another. However, when
you add the interaction with the fourth element,
DECISION MAKING, you get an effect on three other

Self
Machine: elements, plus a normal involvement of the group
             structure's identity element, UNIQUENESS.

             Have you followed what I have done for you?

Inquirer: Yes, I think so.

             Please proceed.

Self   Thank you.
Machine:
             If it is sensible to believe that JUDGMENT, ACTION
             and VISION interact with DECISION MAKING to effect
             the personality elements titled PHILOSOPHY, MEAS-
             URES OF CHARACTER and ROLES, perhaps an approach to
             personality re-construction would involve attention
             to these other three elements and their interaction
             with the element DECISION MAKING. Please consider
             the following 4 x 4 interaction table:

$$
\frac{D}{\begin{array}{c}P\\M\\R\end{array}} \quad
\frac{D}{I} \quad
\frac{P}{J}{I} \quad
\frac{M}{\begin{array}{c}A\\V\\I\end{array}} \quad
\frac{R}{\begin{array}{c}V\\A\\J\\I\end{array}}
$$

             This table suggests that the four personality ele-
             ments DECISION MAKING, PHILOSOPHY, MEASURES OF CHAR-
             ACTER and ROLES so interact that the result is one
             of the three elements you identified as part of your
             problem. Perhaps by attending to those interactions
             you would be able to re-organize your personality by
             effecting changes in the three elements titled
             JUDGMENT, ACTION and VISION.

             Moreover, if you consider the location of these two
             sets of three personality elements at Level II you
             will see that you have shifted from considering a
             PERSON/ENVIRONMENT interaction, in which the problem
             was in the Environment and within you, to consider-
             ing the possibility of an ENVIRONMENT/ENVIRONMENT
             interaction and its possible affect upon you, the
             PERSON.

             Do you understand what I have done?

             Please summarize your understanding of my work to
             this point on your problem.

Inquirer: Yes, I think I understand.

              You have identified for me three unacknowledged por-
              sible sources of my problem. It looks as if while I
              have been understanding my problem, the problem
              within me, in terms of my weakness in making up my
              mind (DECISION MAKING) and my problems with what I
              think I should be (VISION), my difficulty in acting
              (ACTION) and my sense that I have difficulty judging
              what to do (JUDGMENT), there are some other things
              that have been affected and, in turn, have affected
              those other elements. My whole sense of what I be-
              lieve to be the order of things, what is important
              (PHILOSOPHY), my sense of who I am in the world I
              know (MEASURES OF CHARACTER) and the way I relate to
              other people (ROLES) are both affected by my problem
              of making up my mind and, in turn, affect my under-
              standing of the problem.

              Have I understood the implication of what you have
              done for me?

Self   I think so. Your paraphrases of the meanings of the
Machine: several personality elements are reasonably accurate.
              Your inferences of the mutuality of affect also are
              legitimate, in the context of the group structure
              model.

              Would you like me to consider your problem at the
              Level IV.

Inquirer: Yes. That might be interesting.

              Please proceed.

Self   At Level IV you identified constituting elements of
Machine: the constructs PURPOSE, ACTIVITY, PERSISTENCE, and
              KNOWLEDGE as descriptive of your problem. The sec-
              ond interaction table identified that the interac-
              tion of the Level IV constructs KNOWLEDGE, EXPERI-
              ENCE, SOCIETY, and VALUES would tend to result in
              the three constructs PURPOSE, ACTIVITY, and
              PERSISTENCE.

              The Level IV construct KNOWLEDGE is shared by both
              sets of constructs. Part of your problem is a gen-
              eral matter of KNOWLEDGE, apparently. But it is
              only a part of the problem. Do you agree?

Inquirer: I think I do agree.

              Please proceed.

Self Machine:	Thank you.

If you wish to achieve PURPOSE, ACTIVITY and PER-SISTENCE, and if you can see these Level IV constructs as descriptive of your problem, then part of personality re-organization may involve re-organizing your seven interactions between the four constructs KNOWLEDGE, EXPERIENCE, SOCIETY, and VALUES.

Do you follow what I am doing?

Inquirer: No. What are those seven interactions?

Self Machine: The seven interactions referred to are:

KNOWLEDGE and EXPERIENCE,
KNOWLEDGE and SOCIETY,
KNOWLEDGE and VALUES,
EXPERIENCE and SOCIETY,
EXPERIENCE and VALUES,
SOCIETY and VALUES.

Does this help you?

Inquirer: Probably. Will you go to the Level III for me?

Self Machine: Certainly.

At Level III your description of your problem involved Level V constituting elements of the Level III constructs SELF, BEHAVIOR, and FUNCTION. In the second of the interaction tables I identified Level V constitution elements in the Level III constructs of FUNCTION and FIELD. The suggestion to focus on the three newly identified Level V elements translates, at Level III, into a suggestion to re-organize the FUNCTION/FIELD interaction, as a way to achieve an effect upon the Level III constructs of SELF and BEHAVIOR.

Do you recognize your problem in these terms?

Inquirer: Yes, I do. Thank you.

It also suggests another approach to me. Would you check out my thinking for me?

Self Machine: Certainly.

You wish to present me with an idea that you have had as a result of our interchange, and have me use

Self Machine:	my logic analysis capacity to check whether your idea is a logical implication of the group structure model of human personality. I can do that.
	Please tell me your idea.
Inquirer:	Thank you.
	Here is my idea.

(N.B.: At this point the Inquirer and the Self Machine enter into yet another interchange. This imaginative Inquirer/Self Machine dialogue is intended to make but two points. One can imagine, such an interchange, although it is presently easier to imagine a human/human interchange than it is a human/machine interchange. The richness and heuristic capability of the group structure model of human personality has only been suggested in this extended example, but its possibilities exist. The second point, simply put, is that regardless of whether a human/machine interchange is now possible, a human/human interchange becomes possible, given this theoretical perspective. Such an interchange can be a way to help a person understand what is likely to be going on in his own personality and, then, make choices about what changes (if any) he wishes to make.)

We cannot go further in suggesting the way in which persons could interact with the Self Machine to comprehend more and more deeply the process of self-development through decision making. Use of the group structure of Figure 6.1 (See Chapter 6, page 130.) in programming an Information System for Self Decisions accomplishes two things. The process permits monitoring of a person's behavior while interacting with our hypothesized ISSD to ground his or her own self in personality. It also gives us a means to suggest how a person should arrange his or her definitions and experiences to make it possible (through inter-element interactions) to deal with the enlargement of his or her own understanding. These possibilities, combined with those described in Chapter 7, suggest an exciting new human potential.

If individuals adopt the premises of the group structure we have proposed, they have a means within their power to understand how differentiation of new elements of personality emerge in the repeated cycles of integration-differentiation-reintegration that are involved, in a Gestalt fashion, in giving thought-guided direction to activity. Avenues for achieving these possibilities are outlined in Figure 7.2 on page 158.) We would note in Figure 7.1 that the Level VIII elements symbolized as I, a*, b*, c*, d*, e*, f*, and g* become differentiated (that is, enter the level-specific Abelian group structures we have evolved at the Level V elements of Uniqueness, Endowments, Self-Image, Action, and Decision Making. Each of these Level V elements in the group structure is an element in which the person is an initiator of the activity that brings about the differentiation of the element and its presumed subsequent re-intergration with personality in a hierarchical way.

We are excited about this outcome of our exercise. It has re-ordered the elements of a previously incompletely differentiated group and given the re-ordered elements the full power of an Abelian mathematical group. The person _is_ an actual agent in the repeated hierarchical restructuring of the personality through the self when the person is learning. One's avenues of initiative are expressed through one's uniqueness, the evolving knowledge of one's endowments, the images one gives to oneself, the action one undertakes, and the decision making in which one engages.

The fact that the Level VIII generator elements have no independent existence in the Level V column of Figure 7.1 suggests that the mathematical group of which we speak can be conceived as the kind of "open" system we consider to be most like personality itself. The empirical evidence does not currently suggest what those hypothetical Level VIII generator elements might be. However, the properties of the level-specific Abelian groups with which we have been working suggest that such elements do exist. So does Graves' research, apparently, for he proposes eight levels of existential states. It remains for other scientists, psychologists and educators to clarify the requisite structure, perhaps through interaction with our hypothesized Information System for Self Decisions, accepting thereby the properties of the Abelian group we have developed in Section II.

A PROPOSAL: INITIATE AND PLAY
A SELF RESEARCH MACHINE GAME

What currently exists as a Self Research Machine is, we know, trivial. True, there _are_ several programs for interactive numerical analysis, and these go far in helping educational researchers solve problems by relating to their data in more penetrating ways. However, few people have dared to challenge research in terms of its capacity to illiminate the problems and understandings of _persons_, who learn and grow in self-correcting ways as they improve their judgmental functions and

207

structures. Achievement of that objective requires that the powers of numeric analysis be made available to people in general, not just to psychological researchers. Computer programs that give people the capacity to conceive problems as psychological researchers do, when those people are supposed to be in the step of induction in the deciding process while they are learning, would go far to achieve what we call computer-involved living.

Although we are (obviously) far from having a research-grounding personality machine, we think that our analysis implies an interesting possibility for research in the general areas of personality and self. That possibility involves starting with a definition of self research as research that is intended, simultaneously, to inform both the person educating himself or herself and the researcher engaged in the investigation. Furthermore, by acting as if a machine could be constructed which would do such personality research, we believe we would force ourselves to specify, as best we can and whenever we can, what that machine would have to be like. We would need to take the obvious step of acting upon the realization that a computer is not one but many machines and that the writing of procedures is, in effect, the specifying of a machine.

We propose to discipline ourselves to specify a procedure which might elaborate our understanding of giving meaning to research on personality, thereby figuratively closing the logical gap between the two. If this proposal were to be accepted and acted upon however we believe that it would be essential to expose the procedure as well as the understanding. The understanding must be our end product, of course, while the procedure is our means. Our end product (understanding) may look much like a psychology, particularly an embryonic psychology of the tacit mechanism of understanding, including the understanding of personality research itself.

A fundamental premise of our argument thus far has been that not only is accommodation of a particular decision possible but that accommodation of the general decision-making process in a subject or in research itself is also possible. Accommodation of the general decision-making process itself is, we suspect, a phenomenal feat for an individual, both literally and figuratively. By such an accommodation, the content and the process of education (or, for that matter, education's parallel, a self) become one, as J. Bruner (1962) advocated some time ago. Accommodation of the decision-making process itself requires, as we understand it, that one is able to comprehend the principles of design in purpose well enough to deal with them somewhat as objects, even while one is beset on all sides during the decision-making process by their powerful, subjective effects. Moreover, realization of this power seems to

open one to Graves' (1970) interactive life, which is now so
much in demand and so much more frequently present among us.
Reasoning with thought <u>as if</u> there <u>were</u> a machine <u>in</u> Man seems,
to us, to bring this human potential closer to the surface,
closer to actuality, than has heretofore been possible. This
likelihood we regard as most desirable.

Capabilities of the present generation of electronic computers are nearing man-like proportions, although such computers will never <u>be</u> men. However, an understanding of how computers function may raise the question of how much of a
"machine" a man or a woman really is. As we have earlier suggested, comprehension seems to us to reside in questions, not
the question-quieting answers. Therefore, we urge ourselves
and our reader to question in the spirit of Richards, who spoke
of ". . . dividing in order to combine, combining in order to
divide—and simultaneously." (Richards, 1955, p. 18.)

At this point, we must admit that we find ourselves in the
bind that Westin (1970) recently sketched. A new possibility
challenges Mankind. Development and exploitation of that new
possibility promise an equally new comprehension of personality
research, not alone by psychological researchers but also
people generally. However, creation of the actual software and
hardware through which this possibility could find expression
seems to be both a long and an arduous task. A solution of
that task would therefore take the long-term investment of time
and puzzle-solving that Oettinger (1969) recommended for the
general pursuit of technological innovation in educational
forms for the 1970's.

It is also our belief that a solution for the people, the
citizenry, must not exclude the people in its creation. Therefore, it seems reasonable to maintain that a Self Research Machine should undergo further development in the form of what we
would call a Self Research Machine <u>Game</u>. Universities with
their computer centers might well serve as centers for such a
Game. However, playing of that Game must be open to people of
<u>all</u> ages, so that eventual software developed to facilitate the
prosthetic interaction involved in the self-initiated, self-
correcting centering of a self in personal decision making will
remain in the public domain.

We have mapped briefly the types of development which we
think would have to be encouraged for the initiation and playing of what we have come to call a Self Research Machine Game.
The parts for such a Game are around us. The coordination,
leadership, and resources available for common cause are, however, all too evidently <u>lacking</u>. Unfortunately, coordination
and leadership (in the discernibly near future) are <u>not</u> likely

to come from the federal, state, or local governments, or their agencies.

In the present situation, it is incumbent upon persons of vision and those with a vision, to remain steadfast in support of development of a better interactive capacity for learning through and about the self. Two of the most fundamental resources--time and ideas--are readily available. We remain optimistic therefore that students will rally to the idea, especially if the basic "breadboards" of a Self Research Machine Game can be put at their disposal. But to do even that will require money, and that money will probably be hard to get. All the two of us know is that the vision won't come to a person without either the idea or the dream. Therefore, we choose to dream and, in turn, to seek colleagues who will develop similar dreams for the benefit of each man and woman and, through each, of Mankind itself.

We conclude with no easy solution. We have an all too fragile vision, a dream of vastly expanded human freedom and new forms of human responsibility. We can offer no neat, ready-to-use packages that will enable one to do quicker or more efficiently that which has been done less quickly and efficiently up to this time. We can only offer that most abstract, fragile and intangible of things--a possibility, a potential. But we sense that our offer has meaning and direction as its companions. We think that may be all that we humans really need in our education and in our research to enable us to learn to live in a new state of being.

* * * * * * * * * * * * * * * *

BIBLIOGRAPHY

* * * * * * * * * *'* * * * * * *

BIBLIOGRAPHY

Adcock, C. J. Factorial Analysis for Non-Mathematicians. Carlton, Victoria: Melbourne University Press, 1954.

Bell, E. T. Mathematics, Queen and Servant of Science. New York, 1951, in James R. Newman (Ed.) The World of Mathematics. New York: Simon and Schuster, 1956, p. 1534.

Boocock, Sarane. "The Life Career Game," in Personnel and Guidance Journal, 1967, 46, pp. 328-334.

Bruner, Jerome. On Knowing. Cambridge, Massachusetts: Harvard University Press, 1962.

Coleman, James S. Equality of Educational Opportunity. Washington, D. C.: National Center for Educational Statistics, 1966.

Combs, Arthur W. Perceiving, Behaving, Becoming: A New Focus for Education. Washington, D.C.: Association for Supervision and Curriculum Development, 1962, p. 234ff.

Cooley, William W., and Lohnes, Paul. Multivariate Procedures for the Behavioral Sciences. New York: John Wiley, 1962.

Denbow, Carl H., and Goedicke, Victor. Foundations of Mathematics. New York: Harper and Brothers, Publishers, 1959.

Dixon, W. J. (Ed.). BMD Biomedical Computer Programs. Berkeley, California: University of California Press, 2nd ed., 1968, 1969.

Durstine, Richard. "Datafiles for Computerized Vocational Guidance: Requirements, Preparation, Use," in Project Report No. 15. Cambridge, Massachusetts: Information System for Vocational Decisions, Harvard Graduate School of Education, 1968.

Ellis, Allan B., and Tiedeman, David V. "Can a Machine Counsel?" in Wayne Holtzman (Ed.) Computer-Assisted Instruction, Testing, and Guidance. New York: Harper and Row, 1970.

Field, Frank L. Freedom and Control in Education and Society. New York: Thomas Y. Crowell Co., 1970.

Fox, Augustus H. Graphs, Groups, and Games. Boston: Houghton, Mifflin Company, 1970.

Fuller, Frances. The Concerns Model in Teacher Education. Austin, Texas: Research and Development Center in Teacher Education, The University of Texas, 1970. (Multilith)

Fuller, Frances, Bown, Oliver, and Peck, Robert. Creating Climates for Growth. Austin, Texas: The University of Texas, 1967.

Graves, Clare W. "Levels of Existence: An Open System Theory of Values," in Journal of Humanistic Psychology. Vol. X, No. 2, 1970, pp. 131-155.

Guertin, W. H., and Bailey, J. P., Jr. Introduction to Modern Factor Analysis. Ann Arbor, Michigan: Edwards Brothers, Inc., 1970.

Holtzman, Wayne H. (Ed.). Computer-Assisted Instruction, Testing, and Guidance. New York: Harper and Row, 1970.

Hutchinson, Thomas E. Level of Aspiration and Statistical Models Applicable to the Problem of Refining Choice Bases for Career Development. Unpublished doctoral dissertation. Harvard University, Harvard Graduate School of Education, 1968.

Keyser, Cassius J. "The Group Concept," in James R. Newman (Ed.) The World of Mathematics. New York: Simon and Schuster, 1956, p. 1552.

Lefcourt, Herbert M. "The Functions of the Illusions of Control and Freedom," American Psychologist. Vol. 28, No. 5, May, 1973, pp. 424-425.

Ligon, Ernest M. Mathematical Group Theory: A Model for Personality Research. Schenectady, New York: Union College Character Research Project, 1969. (Mimeographed)

Ligon, Ernest M. "A Map for Character Development: Mathematical Group Theory," Character Potential: A Record of Research, Vol. 5, Nos. 1 and 2, July, 1970.

McKeon, Richard (Ed.) The Works of Aristotle. New York: Random House, 1947.

Oates, W., and O'Neill, E., Jr. (Eds.) The Complete Greek Drama. I. New York: Random House, 1938.

Oettinger, Anthony G. Run, Computer, Run: The Mythology of Educational Innovation. Cambridge, Massachusetts: Harvard University Press, 1969.

Piaget, Jean. <u>Logic and Psychology</u>. Manchester: Manchester University Press, 1953.

_____. <u>Six Psychological Studies</u>. New York: Random House, Inc., 1964/1967.

_____. <u>Structuralism</u>. London: Routledge and Kegan Paul, 1968/1971.

Piaget, Jean, and Inhelder, Barbel. <u>The Psychology of the Child</u>. New York: Basic Books, Inc., 1966/1969.

Platt, John. <u>Hierarchical Restructuring</u>. Ann Arbor, Michigan: Mental Health, Research Institute, University of Michigan, 1970. (Multilith)

Polanyi, Michael. <u>The Tacit Dimension</u>. Garden City, New York: Doubleday, 1966.

Richards, Ivor A. <u>Speculative Instruments</u>. New York: Harcourt, Brace and World, 1955.

_____. "The Secret of Feedforward," <u>Saturday Review of Literature</u>, February 3, 1968, pp. 14-17.

Roe, Anne. <u>The Psychology of Occupations</u>. New York: Harper and Row, 1956.

Rulon, Phillip J., Tiedeman, David V., Tatsuoka, Maurice M., and Langmuir, Charles R. <u>Multivariate Statistics in Personnel Classification</u>. New York: John Wiley, 1967.

Sanford, Nevitt. <u>Issues in Personality Theory</u>. San Francisco, California: Jossey-Bass, Inc., Publishers, 1970.

Simon, Herbert. <u>The Sciences of the Artificial</u>. Cambridge, Masssachusetts: MIT Press, 1969.

Skinner, B. F. <u>Beyond Freedom and Dignity</u>. New York: Alfred A. Knopf, 1971.

Thompson, Silvanus P. <u>Calculus Made Easy (Second Edition)</u> New York: Macmillan, 1946.

Tiedeman, David V. "Experimental Method," in Chester W. Harris (Ed.) <u>Encyclopedia of Educational Research</u>. New York: MacMillan, 1960.

_____. "Predicament, Problem, and Psychology: The Case for Paradox in Life and Counseling Psychology," <u>Journal of Counseling Psychology</u>, Vol. 14, 1967, pp. 1-8.

_____. The Cultivation of Careers Through Guidance and Vocational Education. Project Report No. 18. Cambridge, Massachusetts: Information System for Vocational Decisions, Harvard Graduate School of Education, 1969a.

_____. Second Annual Report: Information System for Vocational Decisions. Cambridge, Massachusetts: Harvard Graduate School of Education, 1969b.

_____. Third Report: Information System for Vocational Decisions. Cambridge, Massachusetts: Harvard Graduate School of Education, 1970.

_____. "Self and Hierarchical Restructuring, or Harmonizing the Informing Process and Self." Invited Address, Division E, American Educational Research Association, Chicago, Illinois, April 5, 1972.

Tiedeman, David V., and O'Hara, Robert P. Career Development: Choice and Adjustment. New York: College Entrance Examination Board, 1963.

Tiedeman, David V., and Schmidt, Lyle D. "Technology and Guidance: A Balance," Personnel and Guidance Journal, Vol. 49, 1970, pp. 234-241.

Turing, Alan M. "Computing Machinery and Intelligence." in Mind, Vol. LIX, No. 236, 1950.

Walz, Garry R., and Rich, Juliet V. "The Impact of Information Systems in Counselor Preparation and Prace," Counselor Education and Supervision, Vol. 6, 1967, pp. 275-284.

Westin, Alan F. "Information Technology and Public Decision-Making," in Emmanuel G. Mesthene (Dir.), Harvard University Program on Technology and Society, Sixth Annual Report, 1969-1970. Cambridge, Massachusetts: The Program, Harvard University, 1970.

White, Robert. "Motivation Reconsidered: The Concept of Competence," Psychological Review, Vol. 66, 1959, pp. 297-333.

Williams, Herman. "Serendipity: The Excitement of the Unexpected," Character Potential: A Record of Research, Vol. 5, Nos. 1 and 2, July, 1970, pp. 62-69.

Zinn, Karl L., and McClintock, Susan. Instructional Use of Computers: A Critical Examination with Recommendations for Action. Ann Arbor, Michigan: Project CLUE, Center for Research on Learning and Teaching, 1970.

* * * * * * * * * * * * * * * *

INDEX

* * * * * * * * * * * * * * * *

INDEX

W

Walz, G.R., 216
Westin, A.F., 209, 216
What Is Man?, 69, 159
White, R., 216
Williams, H.J., 78, 79, 216

X

X in a Y
    procedure for, 194

Z

Zinn, K.L., 11, 12, 13, 216

* * * * * * * * * * * * * * * *

A B O U T

T H E

A U T H O R S

* * * * * * * * * * * * * * * *

ABOUT THE AUTHOR

Dr. John Howard Peatling is Director of Basic Research, Union College Character Research Project, Union College, Schenectady, New York.

Dr. Peatling is presently Editor of Character Potential: A Record of Research. His consultant services have included External Evlauation (Research Division), The Support Agency, United Presbyterian Church U.S.A. (NY,NY); Boys Town Youth Research Center, The Catholic University of America (Washington, D.C.); and Workshop in Career Education, Northern Illinois University (DeKalb, IL). In 1972-74 he served as project director of CRP Computer Information System at Union College. He has served as Manager of Management Information Systems for the Episcopal Church (NY,NY) which involved design and initiation of a large system.

Professional memberships include American Association for the Advancement of Science, American Educational Research Association, Association of Professors and Researchers in Religious Education.

Dr. Peatling has made many presentations to various audiences and has written numerous articles published in Character Potential: A Record of Research among which are "A Sense of Justice: Moral Judgment in Children, Adolescents and Adults;" "Cognitive Development: Religious Thinking in Children, Youth and Adults;" "Three Dimen-
sional Research: An Introduction;" "Cognitive Development: A Three Sample Comparison of Means on the Peatling Scales of Religious Think-
ing;" "Cognitive Development in Pupils in Grades Four through Twelve: The Incidence of Concrete and Abstract Religious Thinking in American Children;" and "The Architecture for Self as Its Own Builder." Articles also have been contributed to Religious Education, Learning for Living, The Church Youth, and Sight and Sound.

ABOUT THE AUTHOR

Dr. David V. Tiedeman is Professor of Education at Northern Illinois University, DeKalb, Illinois, and former Director of ERIC Clearing House in Career Education. Throughout his professional life he has contributed to the area of career development.

In 1940 at Harvard University, Tiedeman was involved in translating psychology and psychometrics in the field of education into the practice of guidance and counseling. After earning the Doctor of Education degree, he later joined Harvard's faculty as an Instructor in Education in 1949, and became Professor of Education in 1959, a position he held until 1971. Dr. Tiedeman is a member of numerous professional organizations and has held many offices, having been president of American Personnel and Guidance Association.

Dr. Tiedeman resorted once again to the tentativeness in his commitment to guidance in 1971, leaving Harvard to direct Project TALENT at the American Institute for Research, Palo Alto. In 1973 he returned to the university environment to extend his major interest in career development.

Dr. Tiedeman has spent many years researching career development. An early publication was co-authored with Robert P. O'Hara, CAREER DEVELOPMENT: CHOICE AND ADJUSTMENT: In this

volume Tiedeman outlined a theory of personal decision making in career development. His recent works consist of two volumes. The first, CAREER DEVELOPMENT: EXPLORATION AND COMMITMENT, co-authored with Gordon A. Dudley, provides readers with a comprehensive survey and analysis of many studies and provides readers a primary source document for theory and research in the growing field of career development.

The second in the series, CAREER DEVELOPMENT: DESIGNING SELF, is about knowing self and personality construction theory and offers a design for three successively more complex interactive Information Systems for Vocational Decisions, Educational Decisions and Self Decisions.

Tiedeman Books on Career Development

CAREER DEVELOPMENT: CHOICE AND ADJUSTMENT by D. V. Tiedeman
    and R. P. O'Hara, published by College Entrance
    Examination Board, New York, N. Y., 1963.

CAREER DEVELOPMENT: EXPLORATION AND COMMITMENT by G. A. Dudley
    and D. V. Tiedeman, published by Accelerated Development
    Inc., Muncie, IN., 1977.

CAREER DEVELOPMENT: DESIGNING SELF by J. H. Peatling and
    D. V. Tiedeman, published by Accelerated Development
    Inc., Muncie, IN., 1977.

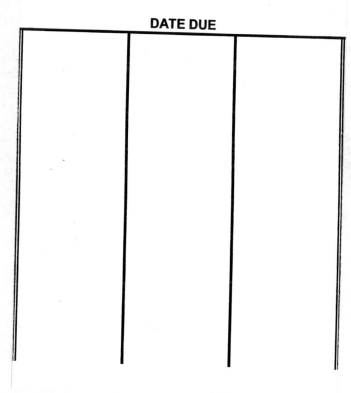

DATE DUE